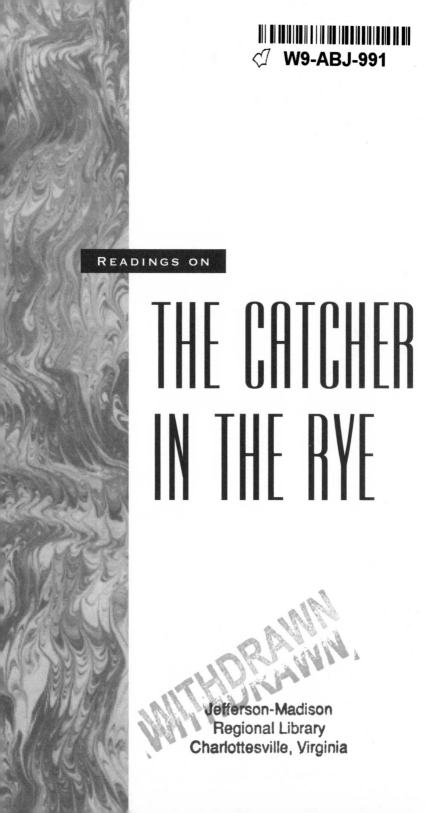

W9-ABJ-991

READINGS ON

THE CATCHER IN THE RYE

WITHDRAWN
WITHDRAWN

Jefferson-Madison
Regional Library
Charlottesville, Virginia

THE GREENHAVEN PRESS
Literary Companion
TO AMERICAN LITERATURE

READINGS ON

THE CATCHER IN THE RYE

David Bender, *Publisher*
Bruno Leone, *Executive Editor*
Brenda Stalcup, *Managing Editor*
Bonnie Szumski, *Series Editor*
Steven Engel, *Book Editor*

Jefferson-Madison
Regional Library
Charlottesville, Virginia

Greenhaven Press, San Diego, CA

1651 6591

L

Every effort has been made to trace the owners of copy-righted material. The articles in this volume may have been edited for content, length, and/or reading level. The titles have been changed to enhance the editorial purpose. Those interested in locating the original source will find the complete citation on the first page of each article.

Library of Congress Cataloging-in-Publication Data

Readings on The catcher in the rye / Steven Engel,
   book editor.
        p.   cm. — (Greenhaven Press literary
   companion to American literature)
     Includes bibliographical references and index.
     ISBN 1-56510-817-5 (lib. : alk. paper). —
   ISBN 1-56510-816-7 (pbk. : alk. paper)
     1. Salinger, J.D. (Jerome David), 1919–   Catcher in
   the rye. 2. Caulfield, Holden (Fictitious character)
   3. Runaway teenagers in literature. 4. Teenage boys in
   literature. I. Engel, Steven, 1968–   . II. Series.
   PS3537.A426C365   1998
   813'.54—dc21   97-43628
                                                               CIP

Cover photo: UPI/Corbis-Bettmann

No part of this book may be reproduced or used in any form or by any means, electrical, mechanical, or otherwise, including, but not limited to, photocopy, recording, or any information storage and retrieval system, without prior written permission from the publisher.

Copyright ©1998 by Greenhaven Press, Inc.
PO Box 289009
San Diego, CA 92198-9009
Printed in the U.S.A.

"What really knocks me out is a book that, when you're done reading it, you wish the author that wrote it was a terrific friend of yours and you could call him up on the phone whenever you felt like it."

—Holden Caulfield

CONTENTS

Chapter 4: *The Catcher in the Rye:*
A Critical Evaluation

FOREWORD

*"'Tis the good reader that
makes the good book."*

Ralph Waldo Emerson

The story's bare facts are simple: The captain, an old and scarred seafarer, walks with a peg leg made of whale ivory. He relentlessly drives his crew to hunt the world's oceans for the great white whale that crippled him. After a long search, the ship encounters the whale and a fierce battle ensues. Finally the captain drives his harpoon into the whale, but the harpoon line catches the captain about the neck and drags him to his death.

A simple story, a straightforward plot—yet, since the 1851 publication of Herman Melville's *Moby-Dick*, readers and critics have found many meanings in the struggle between Captain Ahab and the whale. To some, the novel is a cautionary tale that depicts how Ahab's obsession with revenge leads to his insanity and death. Others believe that the whale represents the unknowable secrets of the universe and that Ahab is a tragic hero who dares to challenge fate by attempting to discover this knowledge. Perhaps Melville intended Ahab as a criticism of Americans' tendency to become involved in well-intentioned but irrational causes. Or did Melville model Ahab after himself, letting his fictional character express his anger at what he perceived as a cruel and distant god?

Although literary critics disagree over the meaning of *Moby-Dick*, readers do not need to choose one particular interpretation in order to gain an understanding of Melville's novel. Instead, by examining various analyses, they can gain numerous insights into the issues that lie under the surface of the basic plot. Studying the writings of literary critics can also aid readers in making their own assessments of *Moby-Dick* and other literary works and in developing analytical thinking skills.

The Greenhaven Literary Companion Series was created with these goals in mind. Designed for young adults, this unique anthology series provides an engaging and comprehensive introduction to literary analysis and criticism. The essays included in the Literary Companion Series are chosen for their accessibility to a young adult audience and are expertly edited in consideration of both the reading and comprehension levels of this audience. In addition, each essay is introduced by a concise summation that presents the contributing writer's main themes and insights. Every anthology in the Literary Companion Series contains a varied selection of critical essays that cover a wide time span and express diverse views. Wherever possible, primary sources are represented through excerpts from authors' notebooks, letters, and journals and through contemporary criticism.

Each title in the Literary Companion Series pays careful consideration to the historical context of the particular author or literary work. In-depth biographies and detailed chronologies reveal important aspects of authors' lives and emphasize the historical events and social milieu that influenced their writings. To facilitate further research, every anthology includes primary and secondary source bibliographies of articles and/or books selected for their suitability for young adults. These engaging features make the Greenhaven Literary Companion Series ideal for introducing students to literary analysis in the classroom or as a library resource for young adults researching the world's great authors and literature.

Exceptional in its focus on young adults, the Greenhaven Literary Companion Series strives to present literary criticism in a compelling and accessible format. Every title in the series is intended to spark readers' interest in leading American and world authors, to help them broaden their understanding of literature, and to encourage them to formulate their own analyses of the literary works that they read. It is the editors' hope that young adult readers will find these anthologies to be true companions in their study of literature.

INTRODUCTION

A brief biographical blurb in Benet's *Reader's Encyclopedia* includes this description of J.D. Salinger: "Perhaps no other writer of so few works has been the subject of so many scholarly analyses." This comment accurately summarizes the world's continued fascination with Salinger's work *The Catcher in the Rye.*

In spite of the many differences between today's adolescents and the fictional Holden Caulfield, Holden seems to typify the adolescent experience. He is dissatisfied with his parents, hopelessly cynical about life and adults in general, yet intrigued by the adult world. A continued favorite in high schools, the novel is used to launch discussion on the meaning of adolescence and the passage into adulthood.

Catcher's enduring success is testimony to Salinger's ability to draw readers in, engaging them in an almost internal dialogue with his books' characters and their dilemmas. Holden could be speaking of the readers of *Catcher* when he explains: "What really knocks me out is a book that, when you're done reading it, you wish the author that wrote it was a terrific friend of yours and you could call him up on the phone whenever you felt like it." Readers certainly feel this type of intimacy not only with Holden, but with other Salinger characters, including Franny, Zooey, and Buddy Glass.

Paradoxically, Salinger has refused to personally forge any intimacy with his reading public. For the past thirty years, Salinger has remained silent, his voice heard only through legal documents and agents' threats. In so doing, Salinger's mystique has grown in direct proportion to his silence, engaging the reader far more than a more accessible man ever could.

Salinger's written legacy is limited to four books: *The Catcher in the Rye, Nine Stories, Franny and Zooey,* and *Raise High the Roof Beam, Carpenters and Seymour: An Introduc-*

tion. Twenty-two short stories remain uncollected and difficult to find.

This literary companion compiles several essays related to *The Catcher in the Rye* that are chosen to enlighten and engage the first-time reader of literary criticism. The articles cover the most commonly discussed elements of *Catcher,* including Holden Caulfield as narrator, and several of the book's themes. In addition, a biographical sketch presents some less well known facts of Salinger's life. A chronology provides a useful overview of Salinger's works and places them in a historical context. The bibliography identifies valuable resources for students completing further research.

Salinger's life and work continue to generate interest and scholarship. Despite his retreat from the public eye, Salinger has remained one of the more influential writers of the twentieth century.

J.D. SALINGER: A BIOGRAPHY

The story of Jerome David Salinger is incomplete and mysterious at best. Only a handful of articles have been written about his life, and the one unofficial biography contains more information about the lawsuit that followed its original publication than it does about Salinger's life. J.D. Salinger's own account of his life is limited to a few comments prefacing his short stories and a small number of interviews; even these are inaccurate and incomplete. Since Salinger last published in 1965, he has been virtually silent. Unlike most of his contemporaries, the reclusive Salinger has avoided the public eye for over thirty years.

SALINGER'S EARLY YEARS

Jerome David Salinger was born on January 1, 1919, to Solomon S. and Marie (née Jillach) Salinger. The couple had a daughter, Doris, born before Jerome. Not much is known about Salinger's early days, although he has said that his "boyhood was very much the same as that of the boy in the book [Holden]." Salinger went to public schools in Manhattan until 1932, when he transferred to the private McBurney School, where he flunked out a year later. His father, perhaps searching for a firm hand to mold the adolescent Jerry, enrolled his son at the Valley Forge Military Academy, a private military prep school in Pennsylvania. At Valley Forge, Salinger was the literary editor of the yearbook, *Crossed Sabres,* became involved in acting, joining the academy's Mask and Spur Dramatic Club, and was a member of the glee club, aviation club, and French club. School records there indicate that he had an IQ of 115.

After graduation in 1936 and taking classes for less than a year at New York University, Salinger traveled to Austria and Poland to help his father's meat importing business and to improve his German. Salinger wrote in the November/December 1944 issue of *Story* magazine: "I was supposed to apprentice myself to the Polish ham business. They finally dragged me off to Bydgoszcz for a couple of months, where I slaughtered pigs, wagoned through the snow with the big slaughter-master. Came back to America and tried college for half a semester, but quit like a quitter." Salinger refers to his brief enrollment at Ursinus College in Pennsylvania, after which he tried his hand at acting. In one of his few interviews, Salinger states that he worked on a Caribbean cruise liner, the MS *Kungsholm*, as an entertainer.

The careers of most successful writers seem to take off at some pivotal date or under some key influence. Nineteen thirty-nine proved to be that year for Salinger—he enrolled in a writing course with Whit Burnett at Columbia University. Burnett, who also published the literary magazine *Story*, later wrote that Salinger stared out the window for most of the class but was the "kind who ingests and then comes out with very edited material." That next year, at the age of twenty-one, Salinger published his first short story, "The Young Folks," in *Story*, the first of four stories that Burnett would publish.

SALINGER AND WAR

Salinger had published four stories before the December 1941 Japanese attack on Pearl Harbor provoked the U.S. entry into World War II. Within weeks Salinger was drafted, reporting for duty in the Army Signal Corps on April 27, 1942. In October 1943 he was transferred to the army's counterintelligence unit. For some time Salinger was stationed in Devonshire, England; on D day, June 6, 1944, he landed on Utah Beach just five hours after the Allies' first assault. His unit's assignment was to cut off communications and interrogate German prisoners.

While in France, Salinger met American author Ernest Hemingway, who was working as a war correspondent. They apparently discussed the relative merits of the German 9 mm luger and the Colt .45 mm pistol, leading Hemingway to demonstrate the effectiveness of one sidearm by shooting off a chicken's head. Salinger was also reported to have carried his portable typewriter around Europe and continued to submit short stories for publication. He wrote to Burnett that he was "still writing whenever [he] could find the time and an unoccupied foxhole." During the war, Salinger managed to publish another ten stories.

Salinger's military service contained more than literary escapades; he went into combat with the Twelfth Regiment of the Fourth Infantry Division in the Battle of the Bulge, one of the largest and bloodiest battles of World War II. The Fourth Division also played pivotal roles in the battle for the Hurtgen Forest and the battle for Luxembourg at the end of 1944.

Although Salinger is not generally thought of as a war writer, a number of his pieces are related to his wartime experiences. Salinger biographer James E. Miller Jr. writes, "We may readily guess that the war was responsible for, or at least brought to the surface, an alienation from modern existence so profound as to maintain itself at times in an overpowering spiritual nausea." Salinger's stories from this time include "Personal Notes of an Infantryman," "Soft-Boiled Sergeant," and "Last Day of the Last Furlough."

AFTER THE WAR

After the war, Salinger remained in Europe on a six-month "civilian contract with the Defense Department." During this time, he married a French physician named Sylvia (her maiden name is unknown). The couple returned to New York in 1946. Although Salinger claimed a telepathic link with his wife, the marriage was short-lived and ended in divorce the next year. Salinger continued to write; between 1946 and 1950 he published ten short stories. Salinger scholar Warren French characterizes many of Salinger's earlier pieces as "very short, highly colloquial, yet heavily ironic tales in the manner made popular by O. Henry." Very few of these stories were republished, even after Salinger became well known, because Salinger saw them as his apprenticeship in the short-story form. Although Salinger questioned the literary merit of these stories, he became increasingly critical of any editing, refusing to allow his stories to be altered in any way. During this time, Salinger focused on publishing in the competitive first rank of literary markets for short-story writers, the so-called slicks, prestigious magazines such as *Collier's*, the *Saturday Evening Post*, *Harper's*, and the *New Yorker*, known for their polished content and professional pay.

Salinger wrote the following about himself for the contributors' notes section in the April 1949 *Harper's:*

> In the first place, if I owned a magazine I would never publish
> a column full of contributors' biographical notes. I seldom

care to know a writer's birthplace, his children's names, his working schedule, the date of his arrest for smuggling guns (the gallant rogue!) during the Irish Rebellion. The writer who tells you these things is also very likely to have his picture taken wearing an open-collared shirt—and he's sure to be looking three-quarter-profile and tragic. He can also be counted on to refer to his wife as a swell gal or a grand person.

I've written biographical notes for a few magazines, and I doubt if I ever said anything honest in them. This time, though, I think I'm a little too far out of my Emily Brontë period to work myself into a Heathcliff. (All writers—no matter how many rebellions they actively support—go to their graves half–Oliver Twist and half–Mary, Mary Quite Contrary.) This time I'm going to make it short and go straight home.

I've been writing seriously for over ten years. Being modest almost to a fault, I won't say I'm a born writer, but I'm certainly a born professional. I don't think I ever *selected* writing as a career. I just started to write when I was eighteen or so and never stopped. (Maybe that isn't quite true. Maybe I *did* select writing as a profession. I don't really remember—I got into it so quickly—and finally.)

I was with the Fourth Division during the war.

I almost always write about very young people.

With these words, Salinger at once both opened the door to speculation and revealed his impatience with people's curiosity about his life.

By the end of the 1940s, Salinger had found an appreciative audience in largely cosmopolitan readers who enjoyed the irony and satire of his stories. Salinger's later work in the *New Yorker* would solidify his position as a writer of literary merit.

SALINGER AND MOVIES

Salinger sought success in Hollywood as well. Former schoolmates remember him hoping to become a screenwriter. In college he wrote film reviews for the school paper, noting in one that he had wanted to throw tomatoes at a Shirley Temple film. His knowledge of film is apparent in *The Catcher in the Rye*, in Holden's comments about a number of contemporary movies. His first Hollywood opportunity came in the late 1940s when producers approached him with an offer to buy the rights to "Uncle Wiggily in Connecticut," a short story originally published in 1948 in the *New Yorker* about a Connecticut housewife whose visit with a high school friend reveals lost love and present indifference. Julius and Philip Epstein, screenwriters of such films as *Casablanca* and *The Brothers Karamazov*, were hired to write the screen adaptation of the story. In 1950, the movie, renamed *My Foolish Heart*, was released starring Dana Andrews and Susan Hayward. The movie received Academy Award nominations for best actress (Hayward) and best song ("My Foolish Heart"). Despite its popular success, the film disappointed Salinger, who has since refused to sell the film rights to any other work. In 1995, however, an Iranian film called *Pari* was released based on Salinger's *Franny and Zooey*.

THE CATCHER IN THE RYE

By 1950 Salinger had established his reputation in the *New Yorker* and his work was already popular among college students. However, it was *The Catcher in the Rye*, the novel he published the next year, that would make him a cultural icon. The publishing company Harcourt Brace originally accepted the book; however, when Salinger was asked to make revisions, he demanded the manuscript's return. Little, Brown then took the book as is, and published it in July 1951.

The Catcher in the Rye was published in the United States with a short biography of Salinger and his photograph on the back cover. His biographical statement reads, in part: "I've been writing since I was fifteen or so. My short stories have appeared in a number of magazines over the past ten years, mostly—and most happily—in *The New Yorker*. I worked on *The Catcher in the Rye*, on and off, for ten years." In fact, six of Salinger's early stories contain references to the Caulfields, including "Slight Rebellion Off Madison" and "I'm Crazy," which were both rewritten into a portion of the novel.

The initial reaction to *Catcher* was somewhat mixed. Critics who were already familiar with Salinger's work responded favorably: Anne L. Goodman wrote in the *New Republic* that the final scene was "as good as anything Salinger has written." However, not all reviewers appreciated the book. Some were put off by the book's language and content. In *Catholic World*, an anonymous reviewer declared that the novel was "monotonous and phony" because of the "excessive use of swearing and coarse language." Ernest Jones wrote that it was the "case history of all of us" and, therefore, boring and predictable. Despite negative reviews, however, *The Catcher in the Rye* continued to sell. By 1961, over 1.5 million copies were sold in the United States. In the decades that followed, the novel remained a favorite of high school and college students. In 1965, *Catcher* sales reached 5 million. By 1975 over 9 million copies of *Catcher* were sold, and in 1986 *Catcher* continued to sell at a rate of twenty to thirty thousand copies a month.

Just as the novel has continued to sell, it continued to gain literary recognition. Arthur Heiserman and James E. Miller Jr., in their article "J.D. Salinger: Some Crazy Cliff," place *Catcher*'s Holden Caulfield in the tradition of literary heroes that includes Ulysses, Aeneas, Jay Gatsby, and Stephen Dedalus. Charles Kaplan, at the same time, published an article comparing *Catcher* and *Huck Finn*, launching a tide of scholarly articles about *The Catcher in the Rye* that would reach its height in the early 1960s. Interestingly, a new—albeit smaller—wave of criticism has recently emerged from non-English-speaking countries, focused on Holden's distinctly American voice and Salinger's use of idioms.

As the critical and popular acclaim for the novel grew, Salinger became more and more reclusive. After the release of the novel, Salinger went to England to avoid publicity. At his insistence, the novel was published in England later in 1951 without the biography and the cover photograph.

On January 1, 1953, Salinger moved to a small rustic cottage in Cornish, New Hampshire. On February 17, 1955, he married Claire Douglas. Surprisingly, Salinger had a large celebration. Later that year a daughter, named Margaret Ann Salinger, was born. Five years later a son, Matthew Salinger, was born.

Nine Stories

Salinger followed the success of *Catcher* in 1953 with the publication of *Nine Stories.* The book quickly hit number one on the *New York Times* best-seller list.

Nine Stories is a collection of seven short pieces that originally appeared in the *New Yorker,* "Down at the Dinghy," first published in *Harper's,* and "De Daumier-Smith's Blue Period," from *World Review.* The stories appear in the order of their publication. These nine stories are colored by Salinger's growing interest in Eastern thought. In fact, the book contains a Zen koan as an epigraph: "We know the sound of two hands clapping. But what is the sound of one hand clapping?" Warren French has written that *Nine Stories* thus carries us through a series of emblematic tableaux of human spiritual evolution—from an opening portrait of a seer whose spiritual insight has completely outstripped his physical discipline ["A Perfect Day for Bananafish"], through the stages as one loses internal vision to gain external control of his body and emotions and then is projected suddenly into spiritual development that provides momentary insights of timelessness, until one is absorbed altogether into the infinite ["Teddy"]. These stories should not be read, however, as models for behavior, but as what James Joyce called "epiphanies" of manifestations of behavior at typical stages in the human fall from glory and reascension back into it.

LATER WORK

Salinger's later work focuses almost exclusively on the seven children of Les and Bessie Glass: Seymour, Buddy, Boo Boo, the twins Walt and Waker, Zooey, and Franny. Four lengthy short stories were collected into two editions: *Franny and Zooey* in 1961 and *Raise High the Roof Beam, Carpenters and Seymour: An Introduction* in 1963. Both collections were immensely and immediately successful.

Franny and Zooey, subjects of the first book, are the youngest of the Glass children. Their tales lack the humor of *The Catcher in the Rye* but more than make up for it in increased depth of theme and philosophical questioning. In "Raise High the Roof Beam, Carpenters," Buddy Glass tells the story of Seymour's failure to show up at his own wedding and charts the reactions of wedding guests, including his own feelings about his brother. The piece begins with the Taoist tale of a horse judge who is able to look beyond the external attributes of a horse and see its "essential" inner qualities. In much the same way, Buddy perceives Seymour's "spiritual mechanism."

One of Salinger's more ambitious stories is "Seymour: An Introduction," a piece of over one hundred pages. In a nontraditional story without a standard narrative flow, the narrator, Buddy Glass, paints a series of portraits of his deceased brother, Seymour. Buddy Glass is a novelist who at times seems to be Salinger's alter ego. Buddy is a story writer and appears to have some of the same frustrations as Salinger. Here Buddy describes his frustration with critics:

> Some people—*not* close friends—have asked me whether a lot of Seymour didn't go into the leading character of the one novel I've published. Actually, most of these people haven't

asked me; they've *told* me. To protest this at all, I've found, makes me break out in hives, but I will say that no one who knew my brother has asked me or told me anything of the kind—for which I'm grateful, and, in a way, more than impressed, since a good many of my characters speak Manhattanese fluently and idiomatically, have a rather common flair for rushing in where most damned fools fear to tread, and are, by and large, pursued by an Entity that I'd much prefer to identify, very roughly, as the Old Man of the Mountain.

Later in the story, Buddy claims to have written "A Perfect Day for Bananafish," further blurring the distinction between Salinger and his narrator.

AFTER HAPWORTH, SECLUSION AND LEGAL ACTION

The Salinger story after his last published work, the short story "Hapworth 16, 1924," is minimal and sketchy. In 1967, Salinger's marriage to Claire Douglas ended in divorce. In 1970, Salinger repaid, with interest, the advance received from Little, Brown for his next novel.

Salinger and his representatives have been very aggressive in protecting his privacy and copyright. In 1974 an unauthorized, pirated collection of unpublished Salinger short stories titled *The Complete Uncollected Stories of J.D. Salinger* appeared. Salinger's attorneys sued bookstore owners who attempted to sell this typewritten compilation of Salinger's early stories.

In 1986 Salinger blocked the publication of Ian Hamilton's *J.D. Salinger: A Writing Life* due to the inclusion of unpublished letters. After a prolonged court battle, Hamilton was ordered to remove the excerpts of the letters, which Hamilton did, publishing the book in 1988. Ironically, the suit against Hamilton resulted in more publicity than the controversial biography might have caused. Salinger's deposition in the Hamilton case did contain a clue to the author's activities over the last twenty years. He commented that he was at work on a project, "Just a work of fiction. That's all. That's the only description I can really give it. . . . It's almost impossible to define. I work with characters, and as they develop, I just go on from there." There has been no other information on this work since.

Salinger's legal actions have not been limited to print; with the advent of electronic media, it has become easier to publish Salinger's work without permission. In 1996 Salinger's agents forced "The Holden Server," a *Catcher in the Rye* website, to remove quotations from the book that appear randomly as people log on. "The Holden Server" complied with Salinger's wishes; it also posted the correspondence between Salinger's agents and the creator of the website, Luke Seeman.

SALINGER AND POPULAR CULTURE

Although Salinger has conscientiously avoided the public eye for decades, his image (or lack thereof) has infiltrated American society, and the absence of the real Salinger has led to speculation, veiled references, and even impostors. As Ian Hamilton puts it, Salinger is "famous for not wanting to be famous." Kurt Vonnegut's *Blackbeard* includes a curmudgeon ex-writer named "Slazenger." In W.P. Kinsella's *Shoeless Joe* (the literary source of the successful Kevin Costner film *Field of Dreams*), the Salinger mystique becomes pivotal to the plot. The protagonist searches out J.D. Salinger and expects to see "a little man with bifocals sitting in an office that smells of furniture polish and floor wax ... holed-up like a badger, on an isolated hill-top in New Hampshire" who "guards his privacy as if it were a virgin bride."

In 1982, Salinger sued a man named Stephen Kunes for impersonation. Two contemporary sitcoms have worked the Salinger mystique in two episodes: Both *The Single Guy* and *Frasier* highlight the fact that although millions have read *The Catcher in the Rye* very few know what Salinger looks like or what he is doing.

SALINGER'S LAST WORDS

In 1997 an interesting new chapter was added to the Salinger story. A small literary publisher, Orchises Press, announced it would reprint in book form Salinger's last short story, "Hapworth 16, 1924." With this announcement, the literary world readied itself for the triumphant return of Salinger. However, in typical Salinger fashion, the book has been delayed for over a year, with the final publication date still in question.

Salinger has left behind one novel and thirteen collected short stories. Deep in meaning and importance, all have inspired innumerable readers who see in them a timeless struggle for purity and spiritual harmony.

CHAPTER 1

Themes and Style in *The Catcher in the Rye*

Zen in *The Catcher in the Rye*

Bernice and Sanford Goldstein

After teaching in Japan, Bernice and Sanford Goldstein returned to Purdue University and published
several studies of the influence of Zen on Western
writers. Sanford Goldstein has also edited a number
of collections of Japanese poets. In this excerpt, the
authors first briefly explain some of the tenets of Zen
and then trace these beliefs through *The Catcher in
the Rye*. They also allude to the further development
of Zen ideas in Salinger's later short stories, especially those dealing with the Glass family.

While it is true that Zen has become a glittering catchword
as connotative as existentialism and at times as meaning-
less, the fact remains that Zen does exist and that Salinger
has shown a definite partiality towards it. Since Zen recog-
nizes that all boundaries are artificial, Salinger's Western experience is not outside the universe Zen encompasses. The
importance of the present moment; the long search and
struggle in which reason, logic, cleverness, and intellect
prove ineffectual; the inadequacy of judgment and criticism
which reinforce and stimulate the artificial boundary between self and other; and some degree of enlightenment
which results from the non-rational and spontaneous blending of dualities, an enlightenment which permits experience
that is complete and unadulterated and makes the moment
and, in effect, life non-phoney—all these aspects of Zen can
be found in Salinger's world.

WHAT IS ZEN?

First, what is Zen and what does the participant in Zen experience? An explanation of the latter may help clarify the
former. The main actor in the typical Zen drama is besieged

Reprinted, by permission, from Bernice Goldstein and Sanford Goldstein, "Zen and
Salinger," *Modern Fiction Studies* 12 (Autumn 1966):313–24; ©1966, The Johns Hopkins University Press.

by doubt and desire. He is not at all certain what enlightenment is, but is convinced it exists, wants it, and is willing to
struggle for it. Believing enlightenment is remote from him
yet intensely desiring it, he pursues it only to find it contin-
ually eludes him. This peculiar dilemma results from the
fact that he believes the search he is making with all his
heart and mind, with all his being and self and ego, is for
something that is *outside* himself. The Zen master, to whom
he has gone for guidance towards the Way, grants him formal interviews with an abundance of ceremony which are
probably intended to make him fully cognizant and thor-
oughly frightened, so the seeker fails in the exercise of the
spontaneous answer to the irrational question, for example,
"What is the sound of one hand clapping?" When not being
questioned by the Zen master, the disciple spends time in
the traditional method of sitting, ponders over various *koan*
or puzzles like the above, and does various tasks with a
minimum of verbal distraction. He is not permitted any of
the temporary satisfactions which give his ego an illusion of
satisfaction or well-being. These pursuits are not done
merely for the sake of subduing or chastising the ego in an
attempt to make it deny itself, but rather to expose the ego
itself as an artificial entity whose very *searching for enlightenment* is spurious.

A number of Zen poems comment on the state of the universe before the disciple began his search: "The mountains
were mountains and the rivers were rivers." During the disciple's search the appearance of the natural world changes,
but once enlightenment comes, the mountains are again
mountains, the rivers rivers. In the same way in the undif-
ferentiated world of early childhood, the separation between
self and the outside world is at a minimum. As Philip
Kapleau says in his book *The Three Pillars of Zen:*

> But what the student responds to most keenly is the visible
> evidence of the roshi's [Venerable Teacher's] liberated mind:
> his childlike spontaneity and simplicity, his radiance and
> compassion, his complete identification with his (the stu-
> dent's) aspiration. A novice who watches his seventy-eight-
> year-old roshi demonstrate a koan with dazzling swiftness
> and total involvement, and who observes the flowing, effort-
> less grace with which he relates himself to any situation and
> to all individuals, knows that he is seeing one of the finest
> products of a unique system of mind and character develop-
> ment, and he is bound to say to himself in his moments of de-

spair: "If through the practice of Zen I can learn to experience life with the same immediacy and awareness, no price will be too high to pay."

Yet for the uninitiated, with the learning of abstractions (language itself being the foremost), self and other are progressively differentiated. Zen's peculiar problem is to bring the self back into a kind of controlled state of infantile non-separation through which it can recognize the arbitrary nature of all the artificial boundaries set up by abstraction and can see the unity in all experience and the existence of ego within that unity. The student seeking enlightenment, therefore, must proceed through his long search and struggle in which reason, logic, cleverness, and intellect prove useless; he must recognize that judgment and criticism reinforce and stimulate the artificial boundary lines of the ego. Finally in the non-rational blending of spurious dualities, he may acquire some degree of enlightenment which will enable him to fully participate in every moment of his day-to-day life. The Zen Master Yasutani-Roshi recites to one of his students the following lines from a famous master: "'When I heard the temple bell ring, suddenly there was no bell and no I, just sound.' In other words, he no longer was aware of a distinction between himself, the bell, the sound, and the universe.". . .

CATCHER FORESHADOWS SALINGER'S LATER STORIES

That Salinger has had Zen on his mind for a considerable period of time can be illustrated by *The Catcher in the Rye,* the germ of the enlightened or to-be-partially enlightened Glass children present there. We find Holden wandering through a lost week-end in which he himself belongs with the phonies. He proceeds from experience to experience, searching for something but always ending up with phonies of one kind or another. At the end of the story, however, Holden, who has had a nervous breakdown (as Franny has) and is being treated in a psychiatric institution, comes to some kind of awareness, namely that he misses all of the "phonies." Holden finally identifies in some way with the people he has spent so much time criticizing, but always criticizing with some degree of sympathy. He is not going to wander off to the West as a blind man or hobo, nor is he going to follow any of the other romantic visions he has toyed with during the course of the novel. Ultimately he is headed toward home. That, of course, is where he does go when he meets his sister Phoebe, and it is Phoebe and the very concrete image of her in her blue coat on a carrousel that ultimately brings Holden to the awareness that he has to go home. The final words in the novel seem to portend the major theme of the Glass stories. A psychiatrist mistakenly asks Holden what he is going to do in September. Holden says he does not know. How should he know what he is going to be doing at such a removed time as next September? Holden seems to imply that he knows what he is doing only at the exact moment he is doing it, not at some point in some arbitrarily designated future.

Holden foreshadows in a much less explicit way the highly critical Glasses, for he too is very clever, very judgmental, very witty, always striving for something. As Salinger proceeds and matures in his career as a writer, what he suggests Holden was searching for becomes more explicit in the Glass stories. Not only is Holden the Catcher in the Rye, as he explicitly tells us—the catcher who catches children before they fall from the field of rye—but Holden too is caught. He is caught in a way quite similar to Buddy's being caught, and that is by the image of love for a dead brother. Holden's brother Allie is intended to be the wise, sagacious Seymour-type. When Holden needs help, he turns to his dead brother Allie. Holden is caught by love and an awareness of something better in the universe, and he is similarly caught by his younger sister Phoebe when she tells him there is nothing in the world he likes. The stress once more is that Holden is far too critical, his critical tendencies similar to those of the Glass trio of Franny, Buddy, and Zooey. Holden's recognition that he has separated himself from all the people he has been defining as phonies comes in his awareness that he misses all of them.

It is this overly critical tendency in Salinger's characters that we want to stress as a key point in Salinger's Zen, and that tendency to be overly critical says something profound about our modern American life, this very critical time of our own very critical people.

The Catcher in the Rye as an Antiwar Novel

John Seelye

Although not a single shot is fired in the novel (in fact, the story takes place during the relatively peaceful postwar America), John Seelye writes that *The Catcher in the Rye* echoes many of the images of the thirties and forties and is a precursor to the antiwar novels of the Vietnam War. Seelye argues that Holden's behavior is modeled on Bogart's movies such as *Casablanca* and *To Have and Have Not*, which act as "pretexts," or indicators to World War II. In addition, Holden's antiestablishment attitudes are the same ones voiced in the Vietnam protests which came fifteen years later. Therefore, *The Catcher in the Rye*, without directly dealing with war, both carries some of the undercurrent of World War II and announces the fears of conscription of the 1960s. John Seelye is a professor at the University of Florida. He has written extensively on American literature, including works on Mark Twain, William Faulkner, and Herman Melville.

Though the novel may be identified with the antiestablishmentarian attitude of fifties intellectuals, who contributed to its popularity, as a deposit of cultural stuff it is demonstrably a product of the forties, the period during which *Catcher* was conceived and written. Incubated during the last years of the Second World War, published in the middle of the Korean War, and having had a definable impact on the literary context of the Vietnam War, *The Catcher in the Rye* is itself a war novel once removed, a subliminal war novel in which not a shot is fired but the process of conscription is well under way....

In returning to Salinger's novel after a hiatus of about

From "Holden in the Museum," by John Seelye, in *New Essays on "The Catcher in the Rye,"* edited by Jack Salzman. Copyright ©1991 by Cambridge University Press. Reprinted by permission of Cambridge University Press.

twenty years, I was struck by the kinds of things I had for-gotten, including some rather remarkable facts, like Holden's height—six feet, two inches—and his patch of grey hair, a Hawthornean blazon on one side of his head. We all remem-ber the red hat, but the grey hair had escaped my memory, and I was, frankly, surprised by Holden's size, having thought of him as, if anything, shorter than average. Except for Frankenstein's monster, most of our archetypal outsiders are not known for superior physical stature, save in moral matters. But the most significant lapse in my memory had to do with what was clearly meant by Salinger as a meaningful characteristic, namely Holden's heavy smoking habit. He smokes several packs a day, according to his own estimate, and the story is spelled out by a steady exhalation of those cigarette-fondling schticks that used to be the standby ges-ture of every short story, novel, and movie script written in the good old days when there was a ready market, not a pro-test line, for stuff with a lot of smoke in it.

THE IMPACT OF BOGART ON HOLDEN

Most important, although Holden frequently dismisses movies with the same snarl with which he defines all the phoniness in the world (both identified with his older brother, D.B.), he has plainly seen a great number of them, to which references abound, and in several scenes he play-acts the part of a dying gangster, crediting the inspiration to "the goddamn movies." Since Holden associates smoking a cigarette with watching "myself getting tough in the mirror," there is a covert, even subliminal suggestion here of Humphrey Bogart as a role model. Nor is it too difficult to conceive of Holden as a first-person narrator derived from those hard-boiled detectives made popular by Chandler and Hammett, who wrote the books that became the movies that made Bogart famous. And since *Breathless* was *the* existen-tial film, Holden stole one on Jean Paul Belmondo also (who actually *does* die from a bullet in the gut), for if *Catcher* is art, then it is Bog-art, and like the characters who made Bogart a famous image, Holden is caught in postures frozen in the forties. Besides the cigarettes and the world-weary pose there is the underworld into which Holden descends after he leaves Pencey Prep, a frozen time frame of 1940s nightclubs, floozies, and pimps, a world as seen over the back of a cab driver, starkly. . . .

Again, the Bogart connection reinforces the extent to which Salinger's is a novel deeply imbedded with forties materials and attitudes. Like the Bogart hero, moreover, the forties was a decade without a distinctive milieu, with very little to call its own, except the Second World War and the Willis Jeep. Cars, costumes, dances, furniture, movies, all were aftereffects of the thirties, furnishing out a long wait for the second explosion of popular culture in the fifties. Salinger's book, I think, draws terrific power from the emptiness of the forties, and if as a decade it was an afterimage of the thirties, then *Catcher* can be read as the ultimate thirties after-story, bereft of the usual social consciousness that characterizes so much fiction of the previous period. Rather than being sustained by some W.P.A.–nourished vision of noble but starving farmers or by the proletarian-novel skeleton that sustains the urban context of a James Farrell or Nelson Algren, Salinger's is a story sustained by the movies of the thirties and early forties, most especially the kind of movie that pitted a noble-hearted detective against the filth and corruption of modern city life or transformed a dying gangster into a religious icon of social inequity. Dropping out of prep school, Holden drops through a crack in time into the reality of the world he knows through movies, and what follows is at once a privileging and a painful critique of the movie myth.

For Holden, the urban world is full of signifiers of adulthood, and he is less eager to rub out the Maurices of that world than he is to stop kids before they enter it, to enlist them in the fate of his favorite brother, Allie, whose mystic catcher's mitt is a creative token opposed to the screenplays written by his other brother in Hollywood. A moviegoer who hates movies, Holden mostly hates adulthood, from which he seeks to rescue all children, much as he wants all the girls he knows to remain virgins. There is of course only one way to escape growing up and that is Allie's way, which is why the book can be read as a lengthy suicide note with a blank space at the end to sign your name. The forties finally was our last great age of innocence, and Holden stands at the exit point, trying to hold everybody back from the fifties. Indeed, it is very difficult to imagine any role for him in the world of television and rock 'n' roll. He is intensely a forties kid, a movie kid, a Bogart boy, and the wonder is the extent to which he could nourish the kinds of kids brought up on television and the Beatles.

The original Holden in one of the early Caulfield stories is reported missing in action in the Pacific during the Second World War, but the boy in the novel is much too young to have served in that war. Still, he is seventeen in 1949 (or 1950, depending on your calculations) just the right age to be drafted into the Korean War, which is the only sequel we can project for Salinger's kid, an obit in a movie-screen epilogue, as at the end of *American Graffiti:*

Holden Caulfield was declared missing in action in Korea.

Which is precisely the fate that awaited a number of kids who identified with Holden in the late fifties and early sixties, only (as after *American Graffiti*) it was in Vietnam. "I swear that if there's ever another war," says Holden, "they'd better just take me out and stick me in front of a firing squad," not because he is a war hater, but because he detests regimentation: "It'd drive me crazy if I had to be in the Army and be with a bunch of guys like Ackley and Stradlater and old Maurice all the time, marching with them and all. . . . I'm sort of glad they've got the atomic bomb invented. If there's ever another war, I'm going to sit right the hell on top of it. I'll volunteer for it, I swear to God I will." If *Catcher* as a narrative is an extended death wish, then underlying that fatalism is an apocalyptic fantasy of self- and universal destruction, illuminating Mr. Antolini's intuition that "I can very clearly see you dying nobly, one way or another, for some highly unworthy cause." We tend to forget the extent to which *Catcher* was written in the shadow of the Second World War, if only because there is scant reference to it, limited to an allusion to D.B.'s noncombatant experience in Europe—"All he had to do was drive some cowboy general around all day." Yet D.B., we are told, "hated the war" and gave Holden *A Farewell to Arms* to read, telling him "that if he'd had to shoot anybody he wouldn't've known which direction to shoot in. He said the Army was practically as full of bastards as the Nazis were," an ideological neutrality not much removed from Joseph Heller's in *Catch-22.*

Holden's account of this conversation ends with the declaration by the mystical Allie that Emily Dickinson was a better war poet than Rupert Brooke, which leaves Holden mystified, but should clarify matters for us. Like Salinger, Dickinson is a death-obsessed writer, whose poetry virtually ignores the Civil War while laying out a bone field that is equivalent to a battlefield after the battle is over. If in D.B.'s declaration concerning the lack of difference between the U.S. Army and the Nazis we have a prevision of *Catch-22,* then in the dialogue between Allie and Holden and in Holden's terror of the army as the ultimate conformist zone we have a subliminal flash of *M.A.S.H.* and *Hair* that explodes into an image of gravestones all in a row upon row. That is, *The Catcher in the Rye* is a text derived from the forties whose post-text was the Korean and hence the Vietnam War. For in Holden we have a boy terrified of regimentation but eager for self- and societal destruction, a true anarchist for whom death is not only preferable to social restraints but the ultimate letting go.

A Subliminal Preparation for War

Bogart's films of the thirties were likewise a subliminal preparation for World War Two, right alongside the C.C.C. camps and other New Deal phenomena of idealistic regimentation, conveying a message concerning the way in which a messy world could be cleaned up, an iconographic cluster centered by the figure of a man holding either a shovel or a gun. It was an idea that gained increasing momentum in *Casablanca* and the movie version of *To Have and Have Not,* featuring cynical American males suddenly motivated to take up arms against a sea full of Nazis. One of Bogart's earliest and lesser-known contributions to the war effort was *Across the Pacific,* set mostly on an ocean liner, with Sidney Greenstreet playing his antagonist, an American university professor so sympathetic to the Japanese people that he is willing to betray his own country. Greenstreet had already figured more famously as the epicene Fat Man in *The Maltese Falcon* (a story virtually without ideology), ironically sharing the name of the bomb that later devastated Hiroshima. *Catcher,* whose pretext is the earlier Bogart films, like those movies lays down the baseline for subsequent conflicts. It provides the rationale not for an anticommunist crusade but for the explosion against the Vietnam War by teenagers unanxious to have their hair cut and their private parts shot off, Procrustean measures associated with the repressiveness of regimentation. At the same time, underlying this anarchistic message there is the essential image of Holden wishing himself on top of the atomic bomb, which evokes that memorable image from *Dr. Strangelove* when Slim Pickens rides down the first shot of World War Three to its Russian target.

This dual nihilistic image is warranted by the pervading gloom of *Catcher,* a Wertherean weltschmerz that provides a threshold for twenty years of death and destruction, much as Goethe's classic of suicide came at the start of the Napoleonic wars. The greatest novel about the Second World War, *The Naked and the Dead,* was built on the thirties-prepared framework of proletarian fiction but with considerable dependence also on a thirties reading of *Moby-Dick* as an antifascist tract. The two most popular antiwar novels that appeared just before or during the Vietnam War, *Catch-22* and *Slaughterhouse-Five,* were set in the Second World War, absurdist fictions that abjured Mailer's doctrinaire third-front framework for surrealistic expeditions into a fatalistic zone. *Catcher* likewise supplied not only the rationale for the antiwar, anti-regimentation movements of the sixties and seventies but provided the anti-ideological basis for many of the actual novels about Vietnam which have been and are still appearing, the early *Catch-22*–inspired fantasies having given way to the dreary, soul-numbing reality of purposeless combat in an empty wasteland of staring eyes.

CATCHER IS A WAR NOVEL

In short, *The Catcher in the Rye* is as much a war novel as is *Moby-Dick,* despite the absence (indeed because of the absence) of an obvious target of bomb-bursting hatred. Appearing in the centennial year of Melville's devastating anatomy of American militaristic/technological culture, which set the whale hunt against the author's personal search for and despair about the meaning and purpose of life, *Catcher* takes place during the same holiday season and provides such an unlikely backdrop to Ishmael's departure. The advent of Christmas is used for ironic effect by both writers, reminding us that the first shots of our entry into World War Two (Salinger's war) also signalled the opening of the Christmas season. *Catcher* is a 'tween-the-wars story without a mad captain or a whale, but American events soon caught up with the book and made good the deficiency, sucking Holden right out of his dark and drizzly December into the maelstrom direct, as the "goddam carrousel" turned into a war machine and Phoebe burst into flame. And now, without a war to give it focus, *Catcher* like *Werther* declines into a tractatus for suicide, which is, as *Moby-Dick* and *M.A.S.H.* both suggest, a reasonable alternative to war, as kids armed with the pistols Holden didn't have hold back saintly rock stars from the corrupting influences of the world by shooting them dead.

The Structure of *The Catcher in the Rye*

Brian Way

Literary critic Brian Way analyzes the tight structure of the novel. Way sees the narrative split into three sections: Holden at Pencey, Holden's escape to New York and his search for sexual adventure, and finally Holden's collapse. Way concludes that the third section is the least successful because Salinger loses the ironic compassion that struck a chord in the first two sections. Way also criticizes Salinger for an unrealistic view of childhood. He finds the novel's strength in the earlier scenes depicting the adolescent's view of the world. Way is the author of *F. Scott Fitzgerald and the Art of Social Fiction.* He has also published pieces on Herman Melville.

The Catcher is not only consistent in tone, but is an extremely well-constructed novel. Beneath its episodic brilliance is a tight three-movement structure. The first movement shows Holden Caulfield at school; the second, his escape to New York and search there for sexual adventure; the third, his collapse, at the conscious level, backward into childhood, at the unconscious forward into madness.

Pencey as a Microcosm

Holden at Pencey Prep can be taken as the young American in his natural setting, a character and a milieu which are strongly individualized and yet in an important sense representative. He is introduced as a complete misfit in the setting which his society considers appropriate for him. School is the agency by which America more than most countries consciously socializes the immature for entry into the approved adult activities: and so a boy's relation to his school becomes a microcosm of the individual's relation to his so-

Reprinted, with permission, from Brian Way, *"Franny and Zooey* and J.D. Salinger," *New Left Review*, May/June 1962, pp. 72–82.

ciety. In this concentration upon a manageable network of representative relationships, we see at work the only method by which a novel can create with any living force the pressures of a society—as opposed to the cinemascope aspirations of a John dos Passos. Holden is hostile to the spirit of his school—

> Pencey Prep is this school that's in Agerstown, Pennsylvania. You probably heard of it. You've probably seen the ads, anyway.

—but also alienated from it: there is his impending expulsion; his losing the fencing foils; above all his relation to the football game—physically remote ('practically the whole school was there except me') and cynical in spirit ('you were supposed to commit suicide or something if old Pencey didn't win').

His detachment from the game is a key to his rejection of the ethos of his society. What depresses and infuriates him most about his headmaster and Spencer is their insistence that 'life is a game'—

> Game my ass. Some game. If you get on the side where all the hot-shots are, then it's a game, all right—I admit that. But if you get on the *other* side, where there aren't any hot-shots, then what's a game about? Nothing. No game.

Games are a system devised for the benefit of the star-performer; the rules of the game enable him to shine, they are no protection for the weak—for those on the side where there aren't any hot-shots. The pretence of team-spirit is pure hypocrisy, and the cynicism of Holden's attitude the proper reaction to the assertion that the game is played for the common good. The game, as seen by Holden, is an image of the competitive society, in its glorification of success, callousness towards failure, and its most unpardonable assertion—that its hotshots not only have the tangible benefits of success but the moral satisfaction of feeling that they are the finest flower of an incorruptible system. Old Ossenburger is the matured product—enormously rich from his cheap funeral parlours; treated with esteem by his society—his old school names a wing after him; and full of moral self-satisfaction:

> The next morning, in chapel, he made a speech that lasted about ten hours. He started off with about 50 corny jokes, to show what a regular guy he was. Very big deal. Then he started telling us how he was never ashamed, when he was

in some kind of trouble or something, to get right down on his knees to pray to God. He told us we should always pray to God—talk to Him and all—wherever we were. He told us we ought to think of Jesus as our buddy and all. He said *he* talked to Jesus all the time. Even when he was driving his car. That killed me. I can just see the big phoney bastard shifting into first gear and asking Jesus to send him a few more stiffs.

The only adequate reaction to him is Marsalla's brief pungent wordless comment. The influence of Ring Lardner is quite evident in this form of broad satiric comedy: Ossenburger is a bloated version of the man from Ogdensburg, New York State, who 'is a Rotarian and a very convicting speaker' (*The Golden Honeymoon*).

The other hot-shot at Pencey is Holden's room-mate Stradlater, an athlete and school hero, 'a very sexy bastard' who is outstandingly successful in the American form of adolescent sexuality—the infantile petting with automobile back-seat as indispensable locale. His fight with Holden over Jane Gallagher brings in the book's other area of concern, the agonies of adolescence. Structurally it is the event which projects Holden into his New York adventures.

HOLDEN'S ATTEMPTS AT SEXUAL SATISFACTION

This second phase is the best part of the book. It describes Holden's four successive attempts at sexual satisfaction: his telephone-call to the girl who is 'not quite a whore'; his evening in the Lavender Room with the three girls from Seattle, Washington; his encounter with the prostitute; and his proposal to Sally Hayes. Salinger captures with extraordinary power, as well as with comic verve, the euphoria of escape from the formal limits of school, and the excited sense of being on the town, with which Holden arrives in New York. Holden's excitement is the excitement of the fantasist: he is embarking on a dream which is both universally adolescent, and built into contemporary American mass-culture through Hollywood and television, advertising, pulp fiction and magazines, and social mores—the offer of unbelievable possibilities of sexual adventure and satisfaction. This erotic day-dream is confronted in each of the four incidents with harsh realities which the day-dream disqualifies the fantasist from handling, in a manner analogous to F. Scott Fitzgerald's Jay Gatsby's experience. Holden is caught in an ironic and painful dialectic: four times his participation in the communal day-dream propel him into real situations from which he recoils, even more incapacitated and humiliated, back into fantasy. The profound pessimism which grows steadily beneath the humour of this movement lies in the fact that the reassuring progressive nineteenth century conviction that one learns from experience is reversed. In a tale like *The Shadow-Line,* for instance, Joseph Conrad shows the young inexperienced commander taking his first ship through a series of difficult situations, and emerging at the end of the voyage matured, and accepted by his mentor, Captain Giles. In *The Catcher,* experience incapacitates and destroys, and after the failure of Holden's last attempt at satisfaction, he is moving towards mental collapse. . . .

HOLDEN'S COLLAPSE ON TWO PLANES

After this, the novel's third phase, the account of Holden's collapse, begins. It takes place on two planes: a conscious groping back towards childhood represented most strongly by his clandestine visit to Phoebe. (The element of unconscious sexual symbolism is clear here—his creeping back into the dark room suggests the womb.) Irresistibly at the unconscious level, he is drifting toward mental breakdown. This part of the novel is much less successful than the two earlier, and contains many of the weaknesses of *For Esmé* and *Franny and Zooey,* both of which offer a number of useful clues to the understanding of the last part of *The Catcher.* Potentialities of mental collapse are suggested much more effectively in the fight with Stradlater, the laughter in New York passage, and the Sally Hayes incident, than anywhere in this last section. There is a general loss of narrative impetus and comic verve: Holden's visit to a movie, though funny, is only a repetition of effects already scored against the Lunts. Salinger's ironic compassion is replaced by a self-regarding, and slightly self-pitying whimsicality which recalls Truman Capote rather than any writer of importance.

His nihilism has a pattern as precise as an equation: Conventional society is a nightmare too horrifying to contemplate—the expensive boarding school, the mockery of family-life, the executive's career, and the call-girl system in *The Catcher;* a respectable marriage in *Uncle Wiggily in Connecticut;* a business-man's adultery in *Pretty Mouth and Green my Eyes.* His despairing analysis does not permit even the stoical resistance of Albert Camus, let alone the positive hope of William Faulkner. The alternatives he presents—

life-in-death conformity and mental collapse—eliminate all possibility of creative living.

In the two earlier phases of the novel, the tensions of this dilemma, fused as they are in a classic portrayal of the contradictions of adolescence, are inescapably challenging. In the last section, however, Salinger's moral analysis of the significance of neurosis is unsatisfying. He slips into the current American habit of equating mental disorder with innocence, recalling Benjy in *The Sound and the Fury;* Augie March's brother George; Dove Linkhorn—a commercialised version in Nelson Algren's A *Walk on the Wild Side;* and Dean Moriarty, the holy goof.

Salinger's Children Are Unreal

More important still is his failure with children, who are not seen with any of his insight into adolescence, but with all the

---

Salinger's Distinctive Style

The language of The Catcher in the Rye *is distinctive.*
Often, reviewers of Catcher *attempt to mimic the vocabulary and rhythms of Holden Caulfield. In this early review of the novel in the July 15, 1951* New York Times Book Review *James Stern attempts to capture Salinger's voice as he relates the plot of the novel.*

This girl Helga, she kills me. She reads just about everything I bring into the house, and a lot of crumby stuff besides. She's crazy about kids. I mean stories about kids. But Hel, she says there's hardly a writer alive can write about children. Only these English guys Richard Hughes and Walter de la Mare, she says. The rest is all corny. It depresses her. That's another thing. She can sniff a corny guy or a phony book quick as a dog smells a rat. This phoniness, it gives old Hel a pain if you want to know the truth. That's why she came hollering to me one day, her hair falling over her face and all, and said I had to read some damn story in the *New Yorker.* Who's the author? I said. Salinger, she told me. J. D. Salinger. Who's he? I asked. How should I know, she said, just you read it. . . .

But I was right, if you want to know the truth. You should've seen old Hel hit the ceiling when I told her this Salinger, he has not only written a novel, it's a Book-of-the-Month Club selection, too. For crying out loud, she said, what's it about? About this Holden Caulfield, I told her, about the time he ran away to New York from this Pencey Prep School in Agerstown, sentimentalizing pre-Freudian unrestraint of a Victorian novelist—the cosiness of Holden's relationship with Phoebe, and his reminiscences of his own childhood visits to the Museum of Natural History. At the same time his children are miniature adults whose opinions gain the factitious piquancy of the pronouncements of Renaissance dwarfs. Esmé is odiously and precociously 'quaint'; Teddy a hateful little Christ disputing with the doctors; all the Glass children were star performers on a radio quiz 'It's a Wise Child'. Salinger's children are as detestable and unreal as Shakespeare's.

His failure here is curiously but closely linked to his success with adolescence: his understanding of adolescent sex is the strength of the earlier passages; his ignorance of the child's relation to sex ruins the close. In the scene where Holden delivers a note to the principal of Phoebe's school and suddenly sees the words '——you' written on the wall, he reflects—

Pa. Why'd he run away, asked old Hel. Because it was a terrible school, I told her, no matter how you looked at it. And there were no girls. What, said old Hel. Well, only this old Selma Thurmer, I said, the headmaster's daughter. But this Holden, he liked her because "she didn't give you a lot of horse-manure about what a great guy her father was.". . .

That's the way it sounds to me, Hel said, and away she went with this crazy book, "The Catcher in the Rye." What did I tell ye, she said next day. This Salinger, he's a short story guy. And he knows how to write about kids. This book though, it's too long. Gets kind of monotonous. And he should've cut out a lot about these jerks and all at that crumby school. They depress me. They really do. Salinger, he's best with real children. I mean young ones like old Phoebe, his kid sister. She's a personality. Holden and little old Phoeb, Hel said, they kill me. This last part about her and Holden and this Mr. Antolini, the only guy Holden ever thought he could trust, who ever took any interest in him, and who turned out queer—that's terrific. I swear it is.

You needn't swear, Hel, I said. Know what? This Holden, he's just like you. He finds the whole world's full of people who say one thing and mean another and he doesn't like it; and he hates movies and phony slobs and snobs and crumby books and war. Boy, how he hates war. Just like you, Hel, I said. But old Hel, she was already reading this crazy "Catcher" book all over again. That's always a good sign with Hel.

It drove me damn near crazy. I thought how Phoebe and all the other little kids would see it, and how they'd wonder what the hell it meant, and then some dirty kid would tell them— all cockeyed naturally—what it meant, and how they'd all *think* about it and maybe even *worry* about it for a couple of days. I kept wanting to kill whoever'd written it. I figured it was some perverty bum that'd sneaked into the school late at night to take a leak or something and then wrote it on the wall. I kept picturing myself catching him at it, and how I'd smash his head on the stone steps till he was good and god- dam dead and bloody.

Salinger is out of touch with the way children actually re- act to obscenity; they accept it either with complete matter- of-factness, or with a delighted relish for the forbidden. The one thing they don't do is worry about it. Salinger is not at all in control of his material here, and although '——you' is represented as being a shock to the children, it is the shock to the rosy, sentimental, backward view of childhood that is in fact resented. The hysterical violence of 'smash his head on the stone steps till he was good and goddam dead and bloody' shows this, and so does the obsessive follow-up, where Holden finds '——you' written up everywhere he goes, and is ultimately convinced that it will be inscribed on his gravestone.

SALINGER'S LOSS OF CONTROL

The fable of the catcher in the rye itself belongs to the same aberrant tendency. Holden wishes to protect children who are playing happily in a field of rye from running over the edge of the cliff that borders the field. Falling over a cliff is a classic unconscious sexual symbol, and here represents without any doubt the dividing-line of puberty, separating the happy innocence of childhood from the dangers and ag- onies of sexual capability. This perpetuates the conventional view of the innocence of children, and shows an atavistic be- lief in the existence of a Fall from grace. It may be objected here that Holden's sexual failures could convincingly make him hanker for a return to a pre-sexual state of existence. If one felt that Salinger were consciously planning this and di- recting one's responses this way, one would agree, but my own feeling is that, by this point in the novel, he is com- pletely submerged in Holden Caulfield and no longer pre- serving that necessary detachment from his main character. Two features of his writing support this view: first, his

abrupt abandonment of his sense of Holden's comic potentialities, expressed earlier in the novel through Holden's tone
of voice as a note of ironically sympathetic self-mockery. It
is this control of tone that gives the prostitute incident, without curbing the farce or minimising the pain its essential
sanity—a dimension which is obviously lacking in the '——
—you' sequence. Secondly, to understand what is happening, one is forced to drag out unconscious sexual symbols
and atavistic superstitions, evidence that the writer has
failed to order his material, and has left in an unrealised
form what he is really writing about—evidence not of pro-
fundity, but of a collapse of artistic control. Such examina-
tions are always impertinent and usually irrelevant, but here
the indications are so unmistakeable, and the connections
with the artistic failure so clear, that one is forced to follow
this line of analysis. In particular, there is the recurring unconscious symbol of a return to the womb—Phoebe's bed-
room (which I have already mentioned); and the Pharaoh's
tomb in the Museum, a peaceful and quiet place which
Holden is hysterically enraged to find violated once again
with the words '——you'.

At the dénouement, Salinger sees Holden Caulfield's
tragic predicament through the kind of closed system which
nihilistic writers construct with diagrammatic clarity: childhood is the only state of existence which is innocent, un-
spoilt, uncorrupted; escape backwards into it is obviously
impossible; the despair of knowing this inexorable situation
is the tragedy. The effectiveness of the tragedy depends on
our accepting the author's view of childhood—a view which
is manifestly false. And so the novel's greatness is flawed by
the dénouement and rests on those earlier scenes of adolescence where there is no falsity of observation, lapse of consciousness, or failure of control.

Symbolism in *The Catcher in the Rye*

Clinton W. Trowbridge

In this piece, Clinton W. Trowbridge argues that the symbolic value of the final episode in the novel can only be appreciated as the conclusion of the larger structure. He believes that Holden has tested several ideal images of himself only to find each of them phony. In the scene with Phoebe in Central Park, Holden again attempts to save his sister from growing up. Although Holden cannot save his sister, he is able to alter his ideal image of the catcher in the rye. He has learned that the world can be loved in spite of its imperfections. Professor Trowbridge teaches English at the College of Charleston. He has written a number of articles on *The Catcher in the Rye.*

As has been generally recognized, *The Catcher in the Rye* is the story of a quest, a search for truth in a world that has been dominated by falsity, the search for personal integrity by a hero who constantly falls short of his own ideal, who, in fact, participates in the very falsity he is trying to escape. The dramatic power of the novel stems from two things: that the hero's conflict is both internal and external and that it increases in intensity as his vision of inner and outer falsity becomes more and more overwhelming. What Leslie Fiedler calls "the pat Happy Ending" is simply the resolution of this conflict, a superbly appropriate one if we take into account what Salinger's intention is.

Thematically speaking, Salinger's intent is to present us with the plight of the idealist in the modern world. The undergraduate's, particularly the idealist undergraduate's, enthusiasm for *The Catcher* shows a recognition of this basic purpose as well as compliments Salinger's rendering of his theme. A college student writes: "Why do I like *The Catcher?*

Reprinted from Clinton W. Trowbridge, "The Symbolic Structure of *The Catcher in the Rye*," *Sewanee Review* 74 (July–September 1966):681–93, by permission of the *Sewanee Review.*

Because it puts forth in a fairly good argument the problems which boys of my age face, and also perhaps the inadequacy with which some of us cope with them. I have great admiration for Caulfield because he didn't compromise. . . . He likes the only things really worth liking, whereas most of us like all the things that aren't worth liking. Because he is sincere he won't settle for less.". . .

What happens to Holden, and what constitutes, therefore, the structural pattern of the novel, is that, as a result of a frighteningly clear vision of the disparity between what is and what ought to be both in the world and in himself and because of an increasing feeling of incapacity to re-form either, he attempts to escape into a series of ideal worlds, fails, and is finally brought to the realization of a higher and more impersonal ideal, that man and the world, in spite of all their imperfections, are to be loved.

FIRST IDEAL IMAGE: SOPHISTICATED ADULT

The first of the ideal worlds into which Holden tries to escape is the sophisticated, man-about-town's New York City, the symbol to virtually every New England prep school boy of the glamorous adult life that his school is the monastic and detested antithesis of. Although Holden is hardly in the right frame of mind to enjoy fully the anticipation of the typical prep school boy's dream—a long weekend on the town—and although he has even seen through this dream, his parting words: "Sleep tight, ya morons!" do represent a complete rejection of the adolescent world. The action that immediately follows reveals Holden trying to play the part of an adult. His first encounter, the scene with Mrs. Morrow, is, significantly enough, his most successful one. He is taken, delightfully, on his own terms. He is allowed to play the man-of-the-world, though only, it is evident, because he is so clearly *playing* it. The rest of his experiences as a man-of-the-world, until that image of himself is destroyed by Maurice, are increasingly unsuccessful. It is his lack of sophistication rather than her unwillingness that is the reason for the failure of the Faith Cavendish affair, but he is refused a drink by the waiter and patronized as well as taken advantage of by the three "grools" from Seattle, screamed at by Horowitz the taxi driver, and treated very much as the younger brother by Lillian Simmons at Ernie's. During these scenes we learn more both about Holden's real affections (his love for the childish innocence and simplicity of his sister and Jane Gallagher) and the degree of his detestation for the very part he is playing and the adult world that he believes insists on his playing that part. Then comes the climactic scene with Sunny and its devastating aftermath.

Maurice's question "Innarested in a little tail t'night?" constitutes a challenge to Holden's image of himself as the suave sophisticate and thus must be answered affirmatively. His subsequent failure with Sunny and the brutality of Maurice's treatment of him are forceful ways of destroying Holden's man-of-the-world image of himself. More important to us, however, is our learning at this point of the nature and degree of Holden's sexual and religious idealism. He cannot use people. Like Christ, he finds pity and compassion to be stronger in him than self-will; unlike Christ, he is unable to find anything in himself approximating to the love of God, anything that can make of this pity and compassion a positive force. And so Holden is merely depressed to the point of contemplating suicide. Already we have the suggestion of what is to become so important later in the novel, that since Holden cannot live up to his Christ ideal, he will choose to emulate the only other character in the Bible he likes, the lunatic "that lived in the tombs and kept cutting himself with stones." It is significant that just as Holden rejected the adolescent world in his parting shout to his dormitory mates at Pencey Prep, so Sunny dismisses his pretensions of being an adult with the wonderfully casual, and completely devastating, "So long, crumb-bum.". . .

SECOND IDEAL IMAGE: THE CATCHER IN THE RYE

With Phoebe, Holden is at home in a world of innocence and integrity. He can trust her to take his side, to understand and sympathize. Thus it is doubly depressing when she reacts in just the opposite manner. Without even being told, she knows that he has been kicked out, and her "Oh, why did you *do* it?" affects him so deeply that he confesses far more than he intends to about the extent of his own nihilistic world-weariness. Phoebe's penetrating "You don't like *any*-thing that's happening" forces him to make some sort of affirmation, to explain the sort of idealism that would justify so sad-making a picture of the world as it is. Neither his affirmation of his love of goodness (his brother Allie, James Castle) nor what might be called his love of pure being (just being with his sister) satisfies Phoebe, but Holden's memory of James Castle, the only person he has ever known who died for a principle, suggests to him a way in which he can devote his life to the protection of goodness. The significance of the catcher image lies in three things. First of all, it is a saviour image, and shows us the extent of Holden's religious idealism. Secondly, it crystallizes for us Holden's concept of good and evil; childhood is good, the only pure good, but it is surrounded by perils, the cliff of adolescence over which the children will plunge into the evil of adulthood unless stopped. But finally, the image is based on a misunderstanding. The Burns poem goes "If a body *meet a body*" not "if a body *catch a body*," and the fact that Phoebe is aware of this and Holden is not, plus the manner in which these two words ("catch" and "meet") are reexamined and re-interpreted by Holden at the end of the novel, shows us in a powerful and deeply suggestive way the center of Holden's difficulty. Both Holden's nihilistic view of life as it is and his notion of what life ought to be are based on a misunderstanding of man's place in the universe. In this central metaphor is condensed the essence of the novel, though not until the end does Holden fully understand the significance of the difference between "man catching" and "man meeting."

Mr. Antolini

Of course, the catcher image does not represent a workable ideal, and Holden knows that. Its very impossibility means that all Holden is left with is his nihilism. He tells Phoebe that he plans to go out West and work on a ranch, but he shows that his real desire is to be saved from the emptiness of his negativism when he telephones Mr. Antolini and when he admits that he almost hopes that his parents will catch him as he sneaks out of the apartment. The catcher, in fact, wants to be caught, the saviour saved.

Mr. Antolini, a former English teacher of Holden's, is the nearest thing that Holden knows to the non-phony adult, and, as such, he is Holden's last refuge. As the person who protected the body of James Castle, he is also to Holden a kind of catcher figure, an image of his own ideal, therefore. In his understanding concern for Holden, and through his remarkably appropriate advice, Antolini does, in fact, seem to be saving him. Holden's physical relaxation, as well as the fact that he seems to have abandoned his plan to run off to the West (he even tells Antolini that he is planning to call up Jane Gallagher in the morning), augurs well for his spiritual recovery. What Antolini tells him, in essence, is that his present depressed state is a perfectly natural result of an awareness of evil, the imperfectness of man and the world, and what he promises him is that if only he will not give up his quest for truth, he will find a way of incorporating his idealism about man and the world into some sort of action, some constructive way of life. His promise that a formal education will help him discover his potentialities—the ways in which he personally can contribute toward the implementation of the ideal—is what he means by discovering the "size [of one's] mind." The phrase, so close to Carl Luce's "the pattern of your mind," represents a wholly contrary idea. It is not adjustment to the world but adjustment to one's self that Mr. Antolini is advocating. With his quotations from Stekel, he is urging Holden toward maturity and a more practical and less egotistical idealism. But then all is ruined by what is basically Holden's intolerance of human imperfection. He is awakened by Antolini's patting him on the head, and once more he rejects what *is* because of its lack of perfection. Pursued by doubts about his interpretation of Antolini's apparent homosexuality as well as guilt feelings about his rejection of Antolini ("even if he was a flit he certainly'd been very nice to me"), he wanders in a state of terrible depression toward literal as well as figurative death.

The literal and figurative coalesce as Holden seems to be plunging into a void each time he crosses the street; he manages to get to the other side only by praying to his dead brother Allie to save him. So terrible is Holden's depression, so complete his sense of alienation from the world of the living, that in his disturbed imagination only the dead, idealized brother can save him from the nothingness, the hellish state of his own nihilism. Resting on a Fifth Avenue bench he comes to a vision of the only ideal world that now seems left to him. Though he does not believe in the serious possibility of the deaf-mute image of himself any more than he did of the catcher figure, it is equally significant as a metaphor of his state of mind. Just as in the catcher image Holden was showing his devotion to the Christ ideal, so in the deaf-mute figure Holden is revealing his allegiance to the only other character he likes in the Bible, the lunatic who lives in the tombs and cuts himself with stones. They are, of course, obverse images of each other: save the world or completely reject it, cherish and protect the good or wall yourself in from the evil, choose health and happiness or the masochistic lunacy of isolation and self-pity. Holden's disillusionment is complete, his search for truth apparently over. He has only to say good-bye to Phoebe and return to her the money she lent him before he starts West. It is as if he were saying good-bye to life itself, a suggestion that Salinger enforces by having Holden almost killed as he runs across the street.

That Holden has given up his idealism, that his decision to go West represents not an escape into an ideal world, as he had formerly thought of it as being, but rather a rejection of his quest, is made clear to us in the next section of the novel. Throughout the novel Holden has been in search of a world, a way of life, an ideal that does not change. What he has never been able to accept is the mutability of life. The images that he loves are static images: Jane Gallagher as the girl who keeps her kings in the back row; children who, because of their absorption in the present and because of their innocence, seem to be unchanging; and above all (and increasingly as the novel progresses) the world of the dead: the martyred James Castle, the idealized, dead younger brother Allie, the natural history museum where even the smells are the same year after year. Holden's absorption with the idea of death reaches its culmination, appropriately enough, in the Egyptian tombs of the Museum of Art. The marvel of the Egyptians was that they were able to achieve permanence with something as essentially impermanent as the human body. The mummies represent the kind of conquest over time and mutability that Holden has been in search of all along. While to the younger boys that Holden is guiding, the tombs are spooky places from which they soon flee, to Holden they are symbolic of the peace and permanence that he so desperately wants. What he discovers there, in the form of the obscenity written under one of the glass cases, is that the quest for permanence is a hopeless one. "That's the whole trouble. You can't ever find a place that's nice and peaceful, because there isn't any." Even death is no escape. The trip West is embraced, but without the usual Caulfield enthusiasm, as a sort of negative ideal. It is the most pathetic, as well as the most fantastic, image of himself that Holden has yet created; and we see how little he is really interested in it, how sadly he must in fact be contemplating it, in the next scene when Phoebe arrives and insists on going with him.

IRONY OF LAST SECTION

The brilliance of the concluding section of the novel lies almost wholly in its irony. The ironic pattern has already been established that each time one of Holden's ideal images of himself is tested by reality it fails and in so failing shows us the phoniness of that particular image. But the images of himself that have been tested thus far have been phony ones and we have been relieved rather than disappointed that he has failed to act in accordance with them. Consider, for example, his behavior with Sunny. Here, for the first time, however, an apparently genuine image of himself is being tested: Holden the non-phony, the only non-phony left, at least in the adult world, is going to preserve his own integrity by keeping himself unspotted from the world and at the same time provide an oasis in the desert of phoniness for those who are worthy of salvation, mainly Phoebe and his older brother D.B. There are remnants of the catcher image in this picture of himself but more significant is the world-weariness, the alienation of himself from all but a chosen few, his apparent contempt for and hatred of the world.

But this too, when tested, turns out to be a phony image of himself. His refusal to allow Phoebe to accompany him, his anger with her for even wanting to go, provides us, and finally himself, with a climactic insight into his real character. In the first place, he is by no means as alienated from his world as he or we supposed. We have believed the theatre to be the epitome of phoniness to Holden; yet what most infuriated Holden about Phoebe's decision to leave with him is that she will not be acting in her school-play if she does. And consider the ironies involved in the fact that the part she is to play is that of Benedict Arnold. He is concerned over whether or not she has had lunch. He tells her that she *has* to go back to school. In fact, we see quite clearly that she is now behaving like him, has taken on his role. This vision of himself, as well as his sudden realization of the extent to which he has endangered the very goodness and innocence that he most wanted to protect, so horrifies him that he immediately abandons his plan to go West, tells her he is going home instead, and carefully and touchingly tries to lead her back to normalcy. Holden, who has apparently been uninfluenced by the various people who have tried to help him in the course of the novel, acts in this scene like a combination of Mr. Spencer, Antolini, and Phoebe as she had been on the previous night. What he tells her even smacks of his headmaster's statement, so abhorred by Holden at the time, that life's a game and has to be played according to the rules.

Secondly, Holden's behavior with Phoebe proves to us the genuineness of the catcher image. When tested, his love for Phoebe and his desire to save her innocence is far greater than his hatred for the world and his determination to abandon it. His love of good is stronger than his hatred of evil. And so, paradoxically, he is saved through saving; the catcher is caught by the person he most wants to catch. Of course, Holden is by no means completely saved, merely reclaimed from the death-like state of his world-weariness. He does, after all, suffer a nervous breakdown. He doesn't know if he's going to "apply himself" or not. Though the conclusion of the novel is hardly a "pat Happy Ending," then, it is affirmative; for Holden has caught some glimpse of how he can implement the catcher image of himself in action and as a result embraces a higher and more impersonal ideal: that man and the world are to be loved in spite of their imperfections.

HOLDEN'S REALIZATION

The experience that leads Holden to this final affirmation occurs while he is watching Phoebe ride the carousel in the zoo.

> All the kids kept trying to grab for the gold ring, and so was old Phoebe, and I was sort of afraid she'd fall off the goddam horse, but I didn't say anything or do anything. The thing with kids is, if they want to grab for the gold ring, you have to let them do it, and not say anything. If they fall off, they fall off, but it's bad if you say anything to them.

Understood in terms of its connection with the original catcher metaphor, what Holden is saying is something like this: innocence and goodness, epitomized in the condition of the child, are not static conditions; just as the child must grow up through adolescence into adulthood, so must innocence and goodness risk this passage through experience and evil. One cannot push the metaphor too far, but the gold ring suggests the promise of life, the beatific end that is the prize as well as the goal. Some are defeated by experience and evil—fall off the horse; others never get the gold ring—fail to attain the promise of life. The important thing to realize is that these are the conditions of life and that (to put it back in terms of the catcher metaphor), rather than attempt the impossible (catch and hold something that by its very nature cannot be caught and held—childhood, innocence), man should meet man, form a relationship of love and understanding with him, and in so doing help him toward his goal just as Holden is doing here with Phoebe. Man cannot save the world; he should not despise it; he may, however, love it. The effects on Holden are immediate.

> I was damn near bawling, I felt so damn happy, if you want to know the truth. I don't know why. It was just that she looked so damn *nice*, the way she kept going around and around, in her blue coat and all. God, I wish you could've been there.

This final sentence sets the tone for the concluding chapter and shows the effect on Holden of his altered catcher ideal. He misses everybody, even Maurice. The concern to communicate, to establish a relationship with man, has led to the love of man. Holden, whose actions and ideas had been prompted largely by his supersensitivity to evil, is now so sensitive to good that he can even love Maurice.

The Catcher in the Rye Is a Cult Novel

Thomas Reed Whissen

Thomas Reed Whissen attempts to identify the sources of *The Catcher in the Rye*'s immense popularity. He notes that the appeal of the book comes from four of Holden's attributes: Holden's way of classifying phonies, his myopic description, his alienation, and his narcissism. These allow the uncritical reader to identify with Holden. Whissen writes that early cult followers of the book believed they were given permission to act as Holden does because they saw themselves in the same "phony" situations as were depicted in the novel. Whissen is professor emeritus at Wright University. He is the author of *Devil's Advocates: Decadence in Modern Literature*.

Ask anyone to name a cult novel and the answer you are most likely to get is *The Catcher in the Rye.* Just as Johann Wolfgang von Goethe's *The Sorrows of Young Werther* is the prototypical cult novel of all time, J.D. Salinger's book is the prototypical cult novel of modern times. The book continues to cast a spell over young readers, and its popularity shows no signs of waning. It has long been required reading in many high school and college English classes, but it has somehow managed to avoid the fate of other books that have been caught in what has been called "the deadly embrace of the academy."

Ian Hamilton, in his unofficial biography of Salinger, says that when he first read *Catcher,* he felt as if he had stumbled upon a book that spoke not just *to* him but *for* him. No one has described the appeal of cult fiction better than this, for a true cult book is one that seems to address the reader directly and to say things in a way the reader would wish to say them. Not all readers, regardless of their enthusiasm, re-

From *Classic Cult Fiction: A Companion to Popular Cult Literature,* by Thomas Reed Whissen. Copyright ©1992 by Thomas Reed Whissen. Reproduced with permission of Greenwood Publishing Group, Inc, Westport, Conn.

spond to this unique book in the same way. While some find Holden Caulfield a lonely misfit worthy of extreme sympathy, others admire his sardonic wit in the face of insurmountable odds. Still others admire his stoicism, for although he has much to resent about the world he inhabits, he accepts its irritations with grace and humor.

THE APPEAL OF THE BOOK

One of the most immediate appeals of the book is Holden's way of classifying people as phonies. Few in the novel escape the label, although Holden does seem to allow for degrees of phoniness. The nuns he meets are perhaps the least phony (except for his dead brother, Allie, and his kid sister, Phoebe), whereas cute little Sally Hayes is described as the "queen of the phonies."

A phony, apparently, is someone who is only out to impress others, someone whose opinions are secondhand, someone who is unable to just "be himself." Just about everyone Holden has any contact with during this three-day sojourn between leaving prep school and arriving home fits into this category. To him, the most pathetic thing about it is that the phonies do not know they are phonies. Holden's own phoniness—his red hunting cap, his lies, his gut-clutching routine—is at least deliberate. His excuse, of course, is that the *real* phonies leave him no choice. Here, however, even he is self-deceived, and it is this gap between self-deception and self-awareness that accounts for the tone of melancholy smugness in the book, arising from what cult readers see as a sad but honest view of the world. . . .

BLURRED EDGES AND DETAILED INTERIORS

Although *The Catcher in the Rye* seems to take place in an easily recognizable world, Salinger is selective in his details in a way that creates a tension between the sharply etched close-up and the vague, impressionistic long-shot. Things like Ackley's pimples, Stradlater's dirty razor, Mr. Spencer's white chest hairs, and the hats the girls from Seattle wear are well-focused and enlarged. Pencey, though, seems to be seen from the hill from which Holden watches the football game. And New York City is not a bustling metropolis full of cars and people but a wintry, desolate place, a murky backdrop against which Holden is dwarfed and isolated. It is eerily quiet and deserted, as if Holden's cab is the only vehicle on the streets and the few people he encounters are the only people in the city.

Even within the vagueness, however, there is precision. Holden's cab may be the only car on the street, but it has a vomity smell to it. An empty hotel lobby smells of 5,000 dead cigars. And when the snow falls, it is like real snow dropped onto a stage setting. Sometimes Salinger creates the opposite effect. When his mother enters D.B.'s room, where Phoebe is sleeping, her presence in this precisely described room is as evanescent as the smoke from the cigarette that Holden has just hastily put out.

When we put these impressions together, we realize that Salinger has created a world of blurred edges and detailed interiors that conveys the illusion of reality but that is actuary a very clever distortion of it. Central Park, for example, is not the park of muggers and bums and assorted vagrants (as it was even then), but rather an empty stage on which Salinger places ducks or children at play or a lonely Holden Caulfield forlornly watching the children and worrying about the ducks. The scene is described with such precision, however, that we accept it without question. It is the reality of perpetual twilight where untroubled children laugh and skate as the sky grows darker and where grim forces that lurk in the shadows prepare to pounce.

HOLDEN'S ALIENATION

Early in the book we see Holden on a hilltop, looking down at a football game in which he has no real interest, either as player or fan. This scene establishes both the fact of his alienation from others and the reason for it. He alienates himself by choice, sometimes because he cannot stand the company of others, sometimes because he becomes disappointed with their company, and sometimes because his actions seem calculated to drive others away.

In all these situations, however, he is ambivalent. He dislikes Ackley and Stradlater, yet seeks them out, only to find further reason for dislike. He visits Mr. Spencer and Mr. Antolini, only to find their company disagreeable. And after forcing himself on Sally Hayes or Carl Luce, he is at pains to be his most obnoxious. His wanting people close to him yet keeping them at a distance is one of the attractions the book continues to have for readers who share his need for people and, at the same time, his distrust of them.

Holden's alienation, however, goes deeper than his ambiguous relationships with people. His family, for one thing, has come apart at the seams. There is no longer a unit he can rejoin. The various educational institutions he has attended promise one thing and do another. Thus, they become things from which he must disengage himself. He cannot tolerate cheap entertainment, yet that which is not cheap is cheapened by those who praise it without understanding it. And even those who do not need to pander to an audience—people like the Lunts and even the Greenwich Village piano player—show off shamelessly. Holden is heading down a road that has only ruts. Twenty years later, in the late sixties or seventies, Holden might have carved his own rut, followed his dream of dropping out and drifting, and nobody would have stopped him or, for that matter, cared. But in his day such a departure was tantamount to social suicide.

Holden is a fledgling existentialist, learning where he is going by going there. He sees that it is up to him to create values in a world that seems to have lost or abandoned its. This is why his frustrated "escape" spoke to those at the time the book appeared who longed for a new direction but simply did not know which way to turn. All they could do was to follow his example and turn inward and risk being called neurotic—or worse.

CULT READERS IDENTIFY WITH HOLDEN'S ADOLESCENT SIDE

Holden Caulfield is too troubled a young man to honestly enjoy feeling superior to others, but many readers see only the brashness and none of the humility. Granted, he is adolescent enough to patronize others at times, but he is also mature enough to know that he, too, is vulnerable. Cult readers, however, identify with the adolescent side of Holden's character without seeing the mature side in true perspective. This reaction is as much Salinger's fault as it is the reader's, for Salinger succeeds almost too well in supplying us with an irresistible way of observing—and abusing—all those phonies who seem all of a sudden to be coming out of the woodwork. Holden's insight seems uncanny for his age, and perhaps the first thing that intrigues us is his precociousness. It makes us wonder why we never saw things so clearly or expressed things so well.

It is easy to see why a cult reader would be overwhelmed by the accuracy of Holden's cold, appraising eye. Even those

readers who are not cult followers find that the book se-
duces them into seeing people through Holden's eyes and
analyzing them as he might. The uncritical reader, however,
has no problem seeing Holden's fits of depression, even his
ultimate institutionalization, as the result of social injustice
rather than personal psychosis. And if that same reader sees
beyond the black humor to the black despair beneath, then
it is easy to see how that reader can feel smugly sympathetic,
nodding in silent commiseration with a fellow victim of life's
callous ironies.

CULT BOOKS REINFORCE THE
READER'S FEELING OF SUPERIORITY

All cult books reinforce the egos of their readers, otherwise
there would be no cult. Cult books are mirrors in which
committed readers see themselves reflected in only the most
flattering sense, in the way Narcissus felt when he spied his
own image in a pool of water, and it was love at first sight.
Cult followers must feel superior to others, and one of the
best ways to feel superior is to be in possession of knowledge
others are too ignorant or too stupid to share. To be able to
convince Mrs. Morrow that her son is an angel when he
knows him to be an obnoxious little nerd is a pleasurable intellectual game for Holden. It is a game his admirers also enjoy, for they become fascinated with the power to manipulate
someone for whom they have no regard. *The Catcher in the
Rye* has encouraged many to enjoy such power by indulging
in similar manipulation. What greater self-satisfaction than
to feel oneself a genuine among the phonies—or better yet, a
"real" phony among all the second-rate fakes?

Although Holden suffers intense loneliness and alienation, and seems to enjoy every painful pang, he also knows
how to make others squirm. His insults range from the subtle and calculated way in which he annoys Carl Luce during
their conversation at the hotel bar to the direct and deliberate way he concludes the afternoon with Sally Hayes by
telling her that she is a "pain in the ass."

The scene between Holden and Ernest Morrow's mother
on the train to New York is an example of manipulation that
is cruelly dishonest. By building up her son in her eyes,
Holden's lies can only result in worse disillusion for the
mother. His premise is that a mother's blindness is phony
and, therefore, worth exploiting.

PERMISSION TO LIE TO "PHONIES"

Although Holden does not seem to think that the sort of lie he tells is destructive, he is quick to pounce on institutional lies ("This school builds character," "You've got to play the game") as slogans that deceive and thus do harm. Such high-handed double-think give cult readers carte blanche to lie and insult whenever they feel they are in the presence of a phony. In fact, cult readers in the fifties got a kick out of "turning somebody on," a phrase that back then meant to put someone on the defensive.

Catcher Is a Weak Novel That Does Not Explore Its Themes Fully

Maxwell Geismar

Influential critic and essayist Maxwell Geismar has written extensively on modern American literature. Although Geismar finds some passages to be well written, he attacks *Catcher* for its failure to answer the questions it raises: Holden Caulfield certainly rebels against the hypocrisy of society, but in what does he believe? Geismar notes that the novel's tone and ambiguous ending are typical of the stories Salinger published in the *New Yorker*.

He worked on *The Catcher in the Rye* for about ten years, J.D. Salinger told us, and when it appeared in 1951, it evoked both critical and popular acclaim. Here was a fresh voice, said Clifton Fadiman in the Book-of-the-Month Club *News*. "One can actually hear it speaking, and what it has to say is uncannily true, perceptive and compassionate." The novel was brilliant, funny, meaningful, said S.N. Behrman. It was probably the most distinguished first novel of the year, said Charles Poore in *Harper's* magazine. The real catch in *The Catcher*, said *Time*, was novelist Salinger himself, who could understand the adolescent mind without displaying one.

Salinger's short stories in the *New Yorker* had already created a stir. In undergraduate circles, and particularly in the women's colleges, this fresh voice, which plainly showed its debt to Ring Lardner, but had its own idiom and message, began to sound prophetic. Salinger was the spokesman of the Ivy League Rebellion during the early Fifties. He had come to express, apparently, the values and aspirations of college youth in a way that nobody since Scott Fitzgerald (the other major influence in his work) had done as well. He is interesting to read for this reason, and because he is a

Reprinted from Maxwell Geismar, *American Moderns: From Rebellion to Conformity* (New York: Hill & Wang, 1958), by permission of the author's estate.

leading light in the *New Yorker* school of writing. (He is probably their *ultimate* artist.) And besides, Salinger's talent is interesting for its own sake.

CATCHER CAPTURES THE SPIRIT OF THE EARLY FIFTIES

But just what is the time spirit that he expresses? The *Catcher's* hero has been expelled from Pencey Prep as the climax of a long adolescent protest. The history teacher who tries to get at the causes of Holden Caulfield's discontent emerges as a moralistic pedagogue, who picks his nose. ("He was really getting the old thumb right in there.") During his farewell lecture, Holden is restless, bored—"I moved my ass a little bit on the bed"—and then suddenly uneasy. "I felt sorry as hell for him all of a sudden. But I just couldn't hang around there any longer." This refrain echoes through the narrative; and the rebellious young hero ends up by being "sorry" for all the jerks, morons, and queers who seem to populate the fashionable and rich preparatory school world.

He is also scornful of all the established conventions as "very big deal." (Another standard refrain in the story.) He seems to be the only truly creative personage in this world, and, though he has failed all his courses except English, he has his own high, almost absolute, standards of literature, at least.

"They gave me *Out of Africa* by Isak Dinesen. I thought it was going to stink, but it didn't. It was a very good book. I'm quite illiterate, but I read a lot." By comparison, *A Farewell to Arms* is really a phony book, so we are told. As in Saul Bellow's work, the very human hero of *The Catcher,* who is a physical weakling, who knows that he is at least half "yellow," is also a symbol of protest against the compulsive virility of the Hemingway school of fiction.

The action of the novel is in fact centered around the athlete Stradlater, who is "a very sexy bastard," and who has borrowed Holden Caulfield's jacket and his girl. Stradlater is "unscrupulous" with girls; he has a very *sincere* voice which he uses to snow them with, while he gives them the time, usually in the back seat of the car. Thinking about all this, Holden gets nervous ("I damn near puked"). In his room, he puts on his pajamas, and the old hunting hat which is his talisman of true rebellion and creativity, and starts out to write the English theme (which Stradlater will use as his own) about his dead brother Allie's baseball mitt. Yet when the athlete returns from his date, full of complacency about Holden's girl and of contempt for Holden's essay, this weakling-hero provokes him into a fight. "Get your dirty stinking moron knees off my chest," says Caulfield to Stradlater. "If I letcha up," says Strad, "willya keep your mouth shut?" "You're a dirty stupid sonuvabitch of a moron," says Holden Caulfield.

Later, nursing a bloody nose as the price of his defiant tongue, he wanders in to old Ackley's room for companionship. "You could also hear old Ackley snoring. Right through the goddam shower curtains you could hear him. He had sinus trouble and he couldn't breathe too hot when he was asleep. That guy had just about everything. Sinus trouble, pimples, lousy teeth, halitosis, crumby fingernails. You had to feel a little sorry for the crazy sonuvabitch." But he can find no comfort or solace in the room which stinks of dirty socks. Ackley is even more stupid than Stradlater. "Stradlater was a goddam genius next to Ackley." A familiar mood of loneliness and despair descends upon him. "I felt so lonesome, all of sudden, I almost wished I was dead. . . . Boy, did I feel rotten. I felt so damn lonesome." He counts his dough ("I was pretty loaded. My grandmother'd just sent me a wad about a week before.") and says good-by:

> When I was all set to go, when I had my bags and all, I stood for a while next to the stairs and took a last look down the goddam corridor. I was sort of crying. I don't know why. I put my red hunting hat on, and turned the peak around to the back, the way I liked it, and then I yelled at the top of my goddam voice, *"Sleep tight, ya morons!"* I'll bet I woke up every bastard on the whole floor. Then I got the hell out. Some stupid guy had thrown peanut shells all over the stairs, and I damn near broke my crazy neck.

THE WEAKNESS OF THE NOVEL

These are handsome prose passages, and *The Catcher in the Rye* is eminently readable and quotable in its tragicomic narrative of preadolescent revolt. Compact, taut, and colorful, the first half of the novel presents in brief compass all the petty horrors, the banalities, the final mediocrity of the typical American prep school. Very fine—and not sustained or fulfilled, as fiction. For the later sections of the narrative are simply an episodic account of Holden Caulfield's "lost weekend" in New York City which manages to sustain our interest but hardly deepens our understanding.

There are very ambiguous elements, moreover, in the

portrait of this sad little screwed-up hero. His urban background is curiously shadowy, like the parents who never quite appear in the story, like the one pure adolescent love affair which is now "ruined" in his memory. The locale of the New York sections is obviously that of a comfortable middle-class urban Jewish society where, however, all the leading figures have become beautifully Anglicized. Holden and Phoebe Caulfield: what perfect American social register names which are presented to us in both a social and a psychological void! Just as the hero's interest in the ancient Egyptians extends only to the fact that they created mummies, so Salinger's own view of his hero's environment omits any reference to its real nature and dynamics.

Though the book is dedicated to Salinger's mother, the fictional mother in the narrative appears only as a voice through the wall. The touching note of affection between the brother and sister is partly a substitute for the missing child-parent relationships (which might indeed clarify the nature of the neurotic hero), and perhaps even a sentimental evasion of the true emotions in a sibling love. The only real creation (or half-creation) in this world is Holden Caulfield himself. And that "compassion," so much praised in the story, and always expressed in the key phrase, "You had to feel sorry"—for him, for her, for them—also implies the same sense of superiority. If this hero really represents the nonconformist rebellion of the Fifties, he is a rebel without a past, apparently, and without a cause.

CATCHER FAILS TO ARGUE FOR A BELIEF

The Catcher in the Rye protests, to be sure, against both the academic and social conformity of its period. But what does it argue *for*? When Holden mopes about the New York museum which is almost the true home of his discredited childhood, he remembers the Indian war-canoes "about as long as three goddam Cadillacs in a row." He refuses any longer to participate in the wealthy private boys' schools where "you have to keep making believe you give a damn if the football team loses, and all you do is talk about girls and liquor and sex all day, and everybody sticks together in these dirty little goddam cliques." Fair enough; while he also rejects the notion of a conventional future in which he would work in an office, make a lot of dough, ride in cabs, play bridge, or go to the movies. But in his own private vision of a better life, this little catcher in the rye sees only those "thousands of little children" all playing near the dangerous cliff, "and nobody's around—nobody big, I mean—except me" to rescue them from their morbid fate.

This is surely the differential revolt of the lonesome rich child, the conspicuous display of leisure-class emotions, the wounded affections never quite faced, of the upper-class orphan. This is the *New Yorker* school of ambiguous finality at its best. But Holden Caulfield's real trouble, as he is told by the equally precocious Phoebe is that he doesn't like *any*thing that is happening. "You don't like any schools. You don't like a million things. You *don't.*" This is also the peak of well-to-do and neurotic anarchism—the one world of cultivated negation in which all those thousands of innocent, pure little children are surely as doomed as their would-be and somewhat paranoid savior. "I have a feeling that you're riding for some kind of a terrible, terrible fall," says the last and best teacher in Holden's tormented academic career. But even this prophetic insight is vitiated by the fact that Mr. Antolini, too, is one of those flits and perverty guys from whom the adolescent hero escapes in shame and fear.

He is still, and forever, the innocent child in the evil and hostile universe, the child who can never grow up. And no wonder that he hears, in the final pages of the narrative, only a chorus of obscene sexual epithets which seem to surround the little moment of lyric happiness with his childlike sister. The real achievement of *The Catcher in the Rye* is that it manages so gracefully to evade just those central questions which it raises, and to preserve both its verbal brilliance and the charm of its emotions within the scope of its own dubious literary form. It is still Salinger's best work, if a highly artificial one, and the caesuras, the absences, the ambiguities at the base of this writer's work became more obvious in his subsequent books.

CHAPTER 2

Influences in *The Catcher in the Rye*

Robert Burns's Poem "Comin' Thro' the Rye" and *Catcher*

Luther S. Luedtke

The title *The Catcher in the Rye* alludes to Robert Burns's poem "Comin' Thro' the Rye." In this article, Luther S. Luedtke discusses how the structure, characterization, and imagery of the poem play out in the novel. Luedtke claims the Burns poem is about a sexual encounter in a field and therefore ties into the theme of innocence and experience in the novel. Dr. Luedtke is president of California Lutheran University. He has published extensively on American literature including *Making American: Society and Culture of the United States.*

The central interpretative problem in *The Catcher in the Rye*—the question of the degree and kind of affirmation or rejection the work ends with—has continued to be open to at least two major contradictory arguments. The one claims that Holden does not change in the novel, that his vision remains statically adolescent; and for its support it points to his nostalgia for a timeless and unfallen toy-world of carousels and blue coats. The other claims that Holden is to emerge from the sanitarium a maturing, potential adult, that, unlike [Mark Twain's] Huck, he will return to the urban East from the garden of the West willing to assume the burdens of adult life, and that this transformation occurs not as a result of psychotherapeutic reconditioning but from Holden's quasi-mystic vision that the way down *is* the way up and from his final acceptance of Christ-like responsibility towards the Maurices, Ackleys, and Stradlaters, as well as the Phoebes, of this world. This position finds its support in Holden's decision to let Phoebe grab for the gold ring, never mind the consequences, and in the kiss and all-absolving

Reprinted, by permission, from Luther S. Luedtke, "J.D. Salinger and Robert Burns: *The Catcher in the Rye*," *Modern Fiction Studies* 16 (Summer 1970):198–201; ©1970, The Johns Hopkins University Press.

rain that follow.

I think, however, that we can largely resolve this interpretative deadlock in favor of the latter, affirmative position by returning to the title of the work itself, following the subtle clues Salinger has left us in Holden's various uses of the title in his narration, and reading more attentively the Robert Burns poem from which Salinger took both title and theme for his novel. It is consistent with our growing awareness of Salinger's conscious craftsmanship in *The Catcher in the Rye* to credit him with this near "total relevance" of source, structure, and innuendo.

THE MISRENDERING OF THE TITLE

The first mention of the title of Burns' poem occurs over halfway through the novel when Holden sees "a little kid about six years old" walking in the street oblivious to traffic and singing "If a body catch a body coming through the rye." At the time Holden did not notice the innocent's happy and secure misrendering of the title, and it made him "feel better." It was the title in this form that Holden first excitedly offered to Phoebe in explaining his chosen role in the world. She checked his enthusiasm, however, by pointing out: "It's 'If a body *meet* a body coming through the rye'!" In this latter passage and those that immediately follow it, Salinger makes two important revelations relevant to the meaning of the novel and to Holden's adjustments.

The first is involved with the temporary change in Holden's narrative stance effected by Phoebe's correction. Although Holden tells his entire story about the "madman stuff" that happened "around last Christmas" in retrospect from a Southern California sanitarium, presumably as part of his rehabilitation, throughout the narration itself he remains faithfully within the time frame of the events narrated, with a few significant lapses into the later perspective of the actual writing-down of his story. The passage following Phoebe's retort is one of these. "She was right, though," Holden said. "It *is* 'If a body meet a body coming through the rye.' *I didn't know it then, though.* [latter italics mine] 'I thought it was "If a body catch a body,"' I said." Here for a moment Holden has stepped forward into the balanced perspective of his post-Christmas rest not merely to confess an earlier factual error but to acknowledge that since "last Christmas" he has grown in knowledge and, we are to assume, in wisdom and understanding. Despite Holden's claim that Mr. Vinson's "Oral Expression" class had not taught him to order his thoughts or to repress his penchant for digression, Holden's narration in *The Catcher* is tightly controlled and progresses with discipline and purpose through its sequence of events. It is out of the same "healed" perspective which makes this ordered self-expression finally possible to him that Holden acknowledges in the passage above that Burns wrote of "meeting" (or, confrontation) rather than "catching" (or, salvation) in the rye.

HOLDEN'S REALIZATION

Holden's final recognition that he cannot be a catcher of children and cannot save them from going off the cliff or from grabbing for the gold ring has, of course, been often recognized and cited, in support both of Holden's final acceptance and of his final rejection of the world. But the intrusion here of the altered perspective of the later Holden, and the internal evidence which this fleeting change in narrative stance offers for final reconciliation, have not been previously explicated. The second major revelation these passages have to make has also escaped notice thus far. It concerns Holden's relation to Phoebe and the differences, not the compatibilities, in the awareness and maturity of the two.

It should be obvious to us from the first Phoebe is not to be identified with the unconscious innocence either of the six-year-old boy or of Holden, for Phoebe already knows, and tells Holden, that in the rye fields of this world bodies are to be met, not saved from falling. In addition, moreover, the action of Burns' poem tells us fully as much about Phoebe as about Holden. Mildred Travis has briefly correlated the kissing, dampness, and crying of Burns' poem to the imagery of the climactic park scene in *The Catcher* [in *Explicator*, December 1962], but she did not, as Salinger—and Phoebe—no doubt had, explore the intention and events of Burns' poem itself. Burns' poem is not a tale of salvation or frozen innocence, but quite the opposite, a tale of seduction and sexual dalliance in the rye—which, we might notice, is to the rye itself far less destructive than children's ball-playing. There is a reason for Jenny's tears and dampness in Burns' poem, for she "draigl't [bedraggled, dirtied] a' her petticoatie/Comin thro' the rye." The dirtying, dampness, crying and tears are, of course, traditional euphemistic symbols of a sexual adventure in the grass, and they place Jenny at the head of a group of "natural" women encompassing, among so many others, not only Thomas Hardy's Tess and William Faulkner's Dewey Dell, Temple Drake, and Caddy Compson (of the soiled underpants), but in due course, we expect, Phoebe as well. It is Phoebe that Holden wants above all others to hold inviolate in the rye field of the children's imaginings, but Phoebe must tell Holden that real rye fields are for private

---

"COMIN' THRO' THE RYE" BY ROBERT BURNS

Scottish poet Robert Burns (1759–1796) wrote both songs and poems in the Scottish dialect. This is the poem Holden incorrectly cites as the source of his idea to be "the catcher in the rye."

> Comin thro' the rye, poor body,
>   Comin thro' the rye,
> She draigl't a' her petticoatie
>   Comin thro' the rye
>
> Oh Jenny's a' weet, poor body,
>   Jenny's seldom dry,
> She draigl't a' her petticoatie
>   Comin thro' the rye,
>
> Gin a body meet a body
>   Comin thro' the rye,
> Gin a body kiss a body
>   Need a body cry.
> Chorus: Oh Jenny's a' weet, &c.
>
> Gin a body meet a body
>   Comin thro' the glen;
> Gin a body kiss a body
>   Need the warld ken!
> Chorus: Oh Jenny's a' weet, &c.

---

meetings, not for universal catchings.

It is through his attitudes towards the various forms of sex that Holden most obviously manifests his nausea of the world. "Sex is something I just don't understand," he tells us early in his narration. "I swear to God I don't." He is repulsed by the touch and wetness of it, yet fascinated by "that girl that was getting water squirted all over her face" in the New York City hotel. Although he is slow to confess it to himself, Holden realizes from the first that even his Phoebe, unlike the young Jane Gallagher, is not meant to "keep her kings in the back row." Holden confesses of Phoebe: "The only trouble is, she's a little too affectionate sometimes." And later he again writes, "She put her arms around my neck and all. She's very affectionate. I mean she's quite affectionate, for a child. Sometimes she's even *too* affectionate. I sort of gave her a kiss."

SIMILAR IMAGERY IN THE POEM AND THE BOOK

But it is Phoebe's genuine love for Holden and her unselfconscious honesty in expressing her affection to him that provide the bridge by which Holden must eventually come to accept love in all its variegations of vision and touch, splendor and squalor. In the final park scene, after Holden has accepted his responsibility for Phoebe and realized his loneliness without her, he can truly accept her kiss, as he had earlier accepted the disembodied grace of her dancing. As if in consequence of this kiss—sad, joyous, prescient and passionate to Holden—it begins to rain, and, like Burns' poem, Salinger's novel ends with ambiguous tears and wet clothes, this time Holden's however, for, although Phoebe's is the instinctual knowledge of woman, in *The Catcher* it is Holden who undergoes Jenny's necessary initiation into the world of the rye. In this moment Holden realizes the beauty of his gain as well as the pathos of his loss, and we can expect that his final response to Burns' rhetorical query, "Gin a body kiss a body/Need the warld ken!", will be a private and appreciative "no.". . .

These elements of narrative structure, source reference, characterization and imagery in *The Catcher in the Rye* suggest that Holden will emerge from his immersion, from his adult baptism, no longer self-consciously innocent and consigned to eternal childhood, like his dead brother Allie, but rather, like Phoebe, free to express and to receive the multitudes of love.

Possible Autobiographical Elements in *Catcher*

Edward R. Ducharme

In this article, Edward R. Ducharme discusses the possible autobiographical elements of Salinger's novel. Because Salinger is reclusive and has been known to provide inaccurate information about his life, the statements that Ducharme makes are, by his admission, assertions that should be read with a critical eye. Nevertheless, Ducharme makes some interesting connections that allow the reader to see *The Catcher in the Rye* as a disguised autobiography. Edward R. Ducharme is the Ellis and Nelle Levit Professor of Education at Drake University. He is also the coeditor of the *Journal of Teacher Education.*

J.D. Salinger is reported to have become very angry when questioned about autobiographical elements in the short story "For Esme: With Love and Squalor." During the conversation that followed he denied that anything he had ever written was autobiographical. On another occasion Salinger authorized the "fact" that he was living in Westport, Connecticut, when he was actually living in Cornish, N.H. Years earlier [in 1945]—writing to *Esquire* in a note accompanying "This Sandwich Has No Mayonaise" (a story in which the death of Holden Caulfield is reported)—Salinger himself asserted that his own Air Corps background had helped in the writing of the story. In the same comment he indicated that he wished to serve in a chorus line after the War was over. W.J. Weatherby, writing in the *Twentieth Century,* quotes Salinger as having said: "It is my subversive opinion that a writer's feelings of anonymity—obscurity, are the second-most valuable property on loan to him during his personal years."

Reprinted, with permission, from Edward R. Ducharme, "J.D., D.B., Sonny, Sunny, and Holden," *English Record* 19 (December 1968):54–58.

LITTLE KNOWN ABOUT SALINGER

The point of all the above is that there is little from Salinger himself on his own life, particularly from 1951 onwards, or, shortly after the publication of *The Catcher in the Rye*. Even those comments given during the earlier years, some of which are referred to above, are a mixture of half-truth and whimsey, difficult sources for the biographer. Yet, in the twentieth century, no man can escape detection altogether; some facts emerge about even the most careful. From those about Salinger can be pieced together a small amount of data relevant to the study of *The Catcher in the Rye* from an autobiographical standpoint. One point must be stressed in reading all of the following: almost every assertion about Salinger's life is from a secondary source and must be regarded as such.

The available facts are as rare and as puzzling as Salinger's stories. There have been several attempts but few successes in the search for facts. Perhaps the most widely used source is William Maxwell's brief biography appearing in the July, 1951, Book-of-the-Month Club *News*. Two of the more ambitious attempts are the *Time* and *Life* articles [Jack Skow's "Sonny: An Introduction" and Ernest Haveman's "The Search for the Mysterious J.D. Salinger"]. These less than complete accounts have received considerable attention. Henry Anatole Grunwald has a lengthy biographical section in his *Salinger: A Critical and Personal Portrait,* the major portion of which is a reprinting of the *Time* and *Life* articles and references to the Maxwell piece. The scarcity of material can be most readily seen when one realizes that even the learned critics have relied upon news magazine articles and a book club notice, sources frequently maligned in literary research. In addition to the above there is a brief passage by Salinger himself in the *First Supplement* to *Twentieth Century Authors*. Finally, one can—if diligent enough—discover a few more things by studying old issues of *Esquire* and *Story* magazines. These are the worthwhile sources.

POSSIBLE AUTOBIOGRAPHICAL ELEMENTS

The attempt to relate the facts to the novel reveals little in the way of extended and extensive material. The simplest facts come first. Salinger and Holden were both born in New York City and spent their early years there. Both attended several secondary schools and left at least one for academic reasons. Salinger attended the McBurney School when he was thirteen, leaving at the end of one year. The McBurney School appears by name in the novel: It is this school that Pencey Prep was scheduled to have a fencing meet with on the day that Holden left the foils on the subway. Related to this point is Grunwald's assertion that Salinger was at one time the manager of the fencing team in one of the schools he attended. Salinger attended the McBurney School because of his parents' concern over his work. Holden was also placed in several schools.

After the McBurney School experience, Salinger went to Valley Forge Military Academy in Wayne, Pennsylvania, the same state in which Pencey Prep is located. The two schools are alike in other respects. Holden speaks of the "crazy cannon" from Revolutionary War days; Jack Skow, in his *Time* story, noted that Valley Forge Military Academy was "heavily fortified with boxwood hedges and Revolutionary War cannon." Holden is wryly amused by the school motto: "Since 1882 we have been molding boys into splendid, clear-thinking young men." The school's pride in its motto is evident in Holden's negative attitude towards it. Both the motto itself and Holden's attitude have probable counterparts. Certainly Valley Forge's motto is similar in intent: "From the embattled fields of Valley Forge went men who built America; from the training fields of Valley Forge go men who preserve America." The 1965 *Handbook of Private Schools* has commercial inserts from over 150 boys schools; only two others in addition to Valley Forge reprint their motto.

There have been some attempts to find the boys who might have served as models for the characters in the novel. Skow states that some like happenings may have occurred at Valley Forge but speculates no further. Grunwald claims that a boy did run away—not Salinger himself, who was too conventional in his revolts for that—and ended up in a West Coast mental institution. He further asserts that another boy committed suicide under circumstances similar to those in James Castle's case. Regardless of the accuracy of such reports, no one has been able to demonstrate that such boys— if they actually did exist—served as models for Salinger.

Both Salinger and Holden had spent some time in Maine during summers. It was in Maine that Holden had played checkers with Jane Gallagher. Skow notes that Salinger had spent several summers at Camp Wigwam in Maine, even being voted the most popular actor.

Other particular places form a common background. Holden speaks of the Museum of Natural History, particularly of the American Indian Room. In a comment to *Story* magazine in 1944, Salinger wrote: " 'I . . . am more inclined to get my New York out of the American Indian Room of the Museum of Natural History, where I used to drop my marbles all over the place.' "

A final note of similarity of Salinger and Holden in young days is revealed by a comment in Skow's piece in *Time.* One of Salinger's schoolboy friends observed that Salinger was always doing slightly unconventional things, the kind of person his own family could not keep track of. Holden's nonconformity is self-evident.

Yet, it is not only as children that relevant likenesses appear. There is the previously mentioned fondness for half-truth and whimsey on Salinger's part. Ernest Haveman, in his article in *Life* tells how Salinger—in his Greenwich Village days during the early fifties—would tell fantastic stories about himself, even convincing one girl that he was the goalie for a professional hockey team. One recalls Holden's fondness for "chucking the old crap around." His entire conversation with Mrs. Morrow while on the train illustrates this point.

The editor's note *Story* magazine in 1944, introducing the story "Once a Week Won't Kill You," tells how Salinger had sent a check for $200 with his story. The check was to be used in some way as a help to young writers. This act of generosity is like Holden's giving money to the two nuns.

The adult Salinger has been much concerned with Buddhism. The two stories "Franny" and "Zooey" contain frequent references; the dedication page of *Nine Stories* contains a quotation from a Buddhist source. Haveman found an ongoing interest in Buddhism at the time of the writing of these works. Towards the end of *The Catcher in the Rye,* Holden speaks of his sister Phoebe as sitting like "one of those Yogi guys."

Phoebe is one of the few whom Holden genuinely likes. She—like Allie and the nuns and James Castle—has a kind of innocence about her that he responds to. Haveman notes that Salinger, in his Village period, had a reputation for dating "the youngest, most innocent kids he could find."

SALINGER, HOLDEN, AND MOVIES

The similarities extend beyond judgment in people. While Holden may have a distaste for some of the things done in films, he nonetheless knows a great deal about them and is quite concerned about certain aspects of filmdom, a side of Holden already well documented. The young and adult Salinger had several relevant experiences with the acting field in general and movies in particular. Young Salinger was so interested in films that he several times expressed the wish of "grabbing the big loot as a Hollywood writer-producer," and "appeared to be intensely interested in getting into the movies or in selling some of his work to Hollywood." The experience at Camp Wigwam has been mentioned; there is, in addition, the evidence that he later specifically mentioned acting as a major interest when being interviewed for the McBurney School. The early Salinger interest is paralleled by Holden's constantly expressing himself in terms of film heroes. The relationship does not stop here, however. Holden is interested in films, but he frequently expresses contempt for them and what they present as well as what they do to the people associated with them. It is in this area that there is a further relationship with the adult Salinger who had some relationship with Hollywood for a brief time.

In 1949 appeared the film *My Foolish Heart* based on Salinger's "Uncle Wiggily in Connecticut," a short story written during the early forties. Salinger's distaste for the film was so great that he has since refused to allow any of his work to be made into films or any plays to be based on his writings. *The Catcher in the Rye* was first published in 1951, two years after the *My Foolish Heart* incident. Thus Holden's distaste for films—despite his considerable knowledge of them—parallels Salinger's. This seems fairly obvious, but there is a more important relationship.

Holden spoke of how his brother D.B. is out working in Hollywood, or as he says, "out in Hollywood . . . being a prostitute." (A further note of parallelism: D.B. wrote a book of short stories in which, according to Holden, the title story called "The Secret Goldfish" is the best. J.D. had, by this time, written and published *Nine Stories;* the most noteworthy in terms of his later preoccupation with the Glass family is "A Perfect Day for Banafish," a title quite like D.B.'s best story. *Nine Stories* also contains "Uncle Wiggily in Connecticut.") The word of importance in Holden's acid description of his brother's activities is *prostitute,* if one is to accept the following.

When Salinger was a teenager and even earlier, his nickname was Sonny. In *The Catcher in the Rye* Holden accepted Maurice's offer to provide a girl for him. While describing his actions while waiting for her and the conversation he has with her, Holden uses the word *prostitute* nine times in reference to the girl. When she arrives, Holden is very reluctant to follow through and engages in what seems like idle conversation. He asks the girl her name and she replies that it is Sunny. Now, it is during these moments that Holden has some of his most discomforting experiences. Salinger— from the evidence available—felt the same way about his film experiences. The real prostitute in the novel, then, has the real name of the real man who had earlier dealt with Hollywood, "being a prostitute," in Holden's words. It is difficult to accept the idea that a writer as perceptive about human beings and as sensitive to language as Salinger is would carelessly give his boyhood nickname to a prostitute, albeit a young one, having already established his adult *alter ego* in the novel as a figurative prostitute.

J.D. Salinger no longer prostitutes himself by having relations with Hollywood. He now lives in near-solitary state in Cornish, N.H. In so doing he is fulfilling one of Holden Caulfield's boyhood dreams: the wish to escape from the world of everydayness to one of undisturbed aloneness. Holden once spoke with Sally Hayes about his wish to live "somewhere with a brook and all." Near the end of the novel, as Holden prepares to run away, he thinks of building a cabin near but not in the woods where he will live by himself with no intrusions from the outside world. Later he says:

> I'd let old Phoebe come out and visit me in the summertime and on Christmas vacation and Easter vacation. And I'd let D.B. come out and visit me for a while if he wanted a nice, quiet place for his writing, but he couldn't write any movies in my cabin, only books and stories.

Comparing *Catcher in the Rye* to *The Adventures of Huckleberry Finn*

Charles Kaplan

Charles Kaplan was one of the first critics to write about the link between Holden Caulfield and Huck Finn. As he notes, both novels share more than the structural similarities of first-person narratives about a boy running away from civilization. In both stories, the young protagonists are on journeys, or quests, to discover themselves, and both attack the hypocrisy of American society. Charles Kaplan taught at San Fernando Valley State College. His other publications include several articles on American fiction, a textbook for composition courses and *The Overwrought Urn*.

Henry Thoreau, himself an interior traveler of some note, says in *A Week on the Concord and Merrimac Rivers:* "The traveller must be born again on the road, and earn a passport from the elements, the principal powers that be for him." In Mark Twain's *Adventures of Huckleberry Finn* (1884) and in J.D. Salinger's *The Catcher in the Rye* (1951) we meet two young travelers—travelers in their native land and also in the geography of their souls. Their narratives are separated in time by almost seventy years, but the psychic connection between them eliminates mere temporal distance: Huck Finn and Holden Caulfield are true blood-brothers, speaking to us in terms that lift their wanderings from the level of the merely picaresque to that of a sensitive and insightful criticism of American life.

Each work, to begin with, is a fine comic novel. Each is rich in incident, varied in characterization, and meaningful

Reprinted from Charles Kaplan, "Holden and Huck: The Odysseys of Youth," *College English* 18 (1956):76–80.

in its entirety. In each the story is narrated by the central figure, an adolescent whose remarkable language is both a reflection and a criticism of his education, his environment, and his times. Each is fundamentally a story of a quest—an adventure story in the age-old pattern of a young lad making his way in a not particularly friendly adult world. An outcast, to all intents without family and friends, the protagonist flees the restraints of the civilization which would make him its victim, and journeys through the world in search of what he thinks is freedom—but which we, his adult readers, recognize to be primarily understanding. Society regards him as a rogue, a ne'er-do-well whose career consists of one scrape after another; but the extent to which he is constantly embroiled with authority is exactly the index of his independence, his sometimes pathetic self-reliance, and his freedom of spirit. He is a total realist, with an acute and instinctive register of mind which enables him to penetrate sham and pretense—qualities which, the more he travels through the adult world, the more he sees as most frequently recurring. He has somehow acquired a code of ethics and a standard of value against which he measures mankind—including, mercilessly, himself. There are some people and things—not many, however—that are (in Holden's term) "nice"; there are many more that are "phony." He does not understand the world, but he knows how one should behave in it. The comic irony that gives each novel its characteristic intellectual slant is provided by the judgments of these young realists on the false ideals and romanticized versions of life which they encounter on their travels.

SIMILAR USE OF LANGUAGE

The slangy, idiomatic, frequently vulgar language which Twain and Salinger put in the mouths of their heroes is remarkable for the clarity of the self-portraits that emerge, as well as for the effortless accuracy of the talk itself. F.R. Leavis describes Huck's colloquial language as a literary medium that is "Shakespearian in its range and subtlety." Likewise, Holden's twentieth-century prep-school vernacular, despite its automatic and somehow innocent obscenities and its hackneyed coinages, also manages to communicate ideas and feelings of a quite complex sort within its sharply delimited boundaries. The language, in each case, is personal, distinctive, and descriptive of character. Holden and

Huck are moralists as well as realists: each has a deep concern with ethical valuation, and each responds fully to the experiences which life offers him. It is the tension between their apparently inadequate idiom and their instinctively full and humane ethics that both Twain and Salinger exploit for comic purposes.

HUCK'S SEARCH FOR IDENTITY

"The traveller must be born again," said Thoreau; and Huck's voyage down the Mississippi is a series of constant rebirths, a search for identity. Beginning with the elaborately staged mock murder which sets him free from the clutches of Pap, Huck assumes a series of varied roles, playing each one like the brilliant improviser that he is. Twain counterpoints Huck's hoaxes against the villainous or merely mercenary pretenses of the Duke and the Dauphin; the boy's sometimes desperate shifts are necessary for his survival and to both his moral and physical progress. The series reaches a climax in the sequence at the Phelps farm, when Huck is forced to assume the identity of Tom Sawyer—when, for the first time, he cannot choose his own role.

This, it seems to me, is a significant variation, pointing to the world which begins to close in upon Huck toward the end of the novel. Not only is an identity forced upon him, but with the appearance of the real Tom Sawyer upon the scene, Huck surrenders the initiative in planning and, in effect, loses control of his own fate. This is the tragedy of Huckleberry Finn: that he has gone so far only to surrender at the end to the forces which have been seeking to capture him. For despite the apparent similarities, there is a vital difference between Huck and Tom: Tom behaves "by the book"; Tom relies on historical precedent; Tom operates within the conventions of the civilized world, accepting its values and standards, and merely play-acting at rebellion—Tom, in short, is no rebel at all, but a romanticizer of reality. Huck's term to describe Tom's method of doing things is that it has "style." Style it may have, but it lacks design. Huck's willingness to let Tom take over Jim's rescue indicates Twain's final acquiescence to the world which has been criticized throughout. True, Huck is going to light out again, he tells us in the last lines: "Aunt Sally she's going to adopt me and sivilize me, and I can't stand it. I been there before." But, despite the expression of sentiments pointing to another future escape—and the fact that the limiting article is not part of Twain's title—Huck, by the end of the novel, has been trapped. I should like to add my bit to the perennial debate concerning the artistic validity of the final sequence, and suggest that it is both ironical and true to life. Tom's play-acting before Huck sets off down the river—his ambuscade of the "A-rabs," for example—seems innocent and amusing; but the rescue of Jim seems, as I think it is meant to seem, tedious and irrelevant. After all, something has happened to Huck—and to us—between chapters 3 and 43.

Huck is trapped by a society whose shortcomings he sees, and he says, "I can't stand it." Holden's terminology is "It depresses me" and "It kills me." Ironically, he is revealed as telling us his narrative from an institution of some kind—psychiatric, we are led to suspect—having also been trapped by the people who want to "sivilize" him.

HOLDEN'S DILEMMA

Holden's instinctive nonconformity asserts itself early in the novel. He has been told by one of the masters at Pencey Prep, from which he is about to be dismissed, that life is a game. "Some game," Holden comments. "If you get on the side where all the hot-shots are, then it's a game, all right—I'll admit that. But if you get on the *other* side, where there aren't any hot-shots, then what's a game about it. Nothing. No game." At the age of seventeen he has learned to suspect the glib philosophies of his elders, and to test the coil of experience by determining whether it rings true or false for him, personally.

Like Huck, Holden is also a refugee. He flees the campus of Pencey Prep before he is formally expelled, and returns to New York City to have three days of freedom before rejoining his family. Pencey Prep is merely the most recent in a series of unsatisfactory academic experiences for him. "One of the biggest reasons I left Elkton Hills was because I was surrounded by phonies. That's all. They were coming in the goddam window. I can't stand that stuff. It drives me crazy. It makes me so depressed I go crazy."

Also like Huck, Holden assumes a series of guises during his lone wanderings. "I'm the most terrific liar you ever saw in your life. It's awful. If I'm on the way to the store to buy a magazine, even, and somebody asks me where I'm going. I'm liable to say I'm going to the opera. It's terrible." In a sequence which reminds one forcibly of Huck Finn. Holden finds himself in conversation with the mother of one of his classmates, Ernie Morrow, whom he describes as "doubtless the biggest bastard that ever went to Pencey, in the whole crumby history of the school." But Holden, adopting the name of "Rudolf Schmidt" (the janitor), tells her what she wants to hear about her son, to her wonder and delight. Holden's comment is: "Mothers are all slightly insane. The thing is, though, I liked old Morrow's mother. She was all right." His imagination rampant, Holden tells her a cock-and-bull story which includes an impending brain operation and a trip to South America to visit his grandmother, but he stops just short of revealing himself completely. It is a wonderfully funny scene, showing Holden in several aspects: his instinctive evaluation of the mother's "rightness" overcoming his profound distaste for her son, his adolescent imagination in a frenzy of wild invention, and his own awareness of the limits to which he can act his suddenly-adopted role of Rudolf Schmidt.

TESTS FOR BOTH CHARACTERS

Huck's tortured decision not to "turn in" Jim is made on the basis of his own feelings, which he automatically assumes to be sinful since they have so often put him at odds with society. His personal moral code seems always to run counter to his duty to society, a conflict which serves to confirm him in the belief that wickedness is in his line, "being brung up to it." In the crucial moral act of the novel, Huck must "decide, forever, betwixt two things, and I knowed it. I studied a minute, sort of holding my breath, and then says to myself, 'All right, then I'll *go* to hell.'" Huck's humanity overcomes the so-called duty to society. Holden, also, is "depressed" by the notion that he is somehow a misfit, that he does strange, irrational things, that he is fighting a constant war with society—but his awareness of his own weaknesses (his compulsive lying, for example) is the result of his searching honesty.

The yardstick which Holden applies to the world is a simple one—too simple, perhaps, too rigorous, too uncompromising, for anyone but an adolescent (or, as the popular phrase has it, "a crazy mixed-up kid") to attempt to apply to a complex world: it is the test of truth. The world is full of phonies—so Holden dreams of running away and building his own cabin, where people would come and visit him. "I'd have this rule that nobody could do anything phony when they visited me. If anybody tried to do anything phony, they couldn't stay."

SIMILAR WORLDS

Huck's world, realistically depicted as mid-America in the middle of the nineteenth century, is also the world where the established codes are penetrated as being either hypocritical or superficial; Huck finds peace and reassurance away from the haunts of man, out on the river. After the waste and folly of the Grangerford-Shepherdson sequence, for example, Huck retreats to the river:

> Sometimes we'd have that whole river all to ourselves for the longest time. Yonder was the banks and the islands, across the water; and maybe a spark—which was a candle in a cabin window; and sometimes on the water you could see a spark or two—on a raft or a scow, you know; and maybe you could hear a fiddle or a song coming over from one of them crafts. It's lovely to live on a raft.

But the idyll is interrupted shortly thereafter with "a couple of men tearing up the path as tight as they could foot it"—the Duke and the Dauphin imposing their unsavory world upon Huck's.

HOLDEN'S PHONY WORLD

Holden's world is post-war New York City, from the Metropolitan Museum to Greenwich Village, during Christmas week, where, in successive incidents, he encounters pompous hypocrisy, ignorance, indifference, moral corruption, sexual perversion, and—pervading all—"phoniness." Holden's older brother, a once promising writer, is now a Hollywood scenarist; the corruption of his talent is symptomatic to Holden of the general influence of the movies: "They can ruin you. I'm not kidding." They represent the world at its "phoniest" in their falsification of reality; in addition, they corrupt their audiences, converting them into people like the three pathetic girls from Seattle who spend all evening in a second-rate night club looking for movie stars, or like the woman Holden observes at the Radio City Music Hall. She cries through the entire picture, and "the phonier it got, the more she cried. . . . She had this little kid with her that was bored as hell and had to go to the bathroom, but she wouldn't take him. . . . She was about as kind-hearted as a goddam wolf."

Holden's awareness of sham sensitizes him to its manifestations wherever it appears: in the pseudo-religious Christmas spectacle at Radio City ("I can't see anything religious or pretty, for God's sake, about a bunch of actors carrying crucifixes all over the stage"); in ministers with "Holy Joe" voices; in magazine fiction, with its "lean-jawed guys named David" and "phony girls named Linda or Marcia"; and in the performance of a gifted night-club pianist as well as that of the Lunts. His reaction to the performances of all three is a comment on the relationship between virtuosity and integrity: "If you do something *too* good, then, after a while, if you don't watch it, you start showing off. And then you're not as good any more." Both mock humility and casual bravura are dangerous to the integrity of the individual: Holden finds no "naturalness" in the finished and most artistic performers in his world. His world, he comes to feel, is full of obscenities, both figurative and actual; even a million years would be inadequate to erase all the obscenities scribbled on all the walls. His week-end in New York reminds him of the time an alumnus of Pencey visited the school and inspected the doors in the men's toilet to see if his initials were still carved there. While he searched for this memento of his past, he solemnly gave platitudinous advice to the boys. The glaring disparity between what even "good guys" say and what they do is enough to make Holden despair of finding anyone, except his sister Phoebe, with whom he can communicate honestly.

A few things Holden encounters on his voyage through the metropolis make him "feel better." Like Huck, who has to retreat regularly to the river, to reestablish his contacts with his sources of value, Holden several times meets perfectly "natural" things which delight him: the kettle-drummer in the orchestra, who never looks bored, but who bangs his drums "so nice and sweet, with this nervous expression on his face"; a Dixieland song recorded by a Negro girl who doesn't make it sound "mushy" or "cute"; and the sight of a family coming out of church. But these incidents merely serve to reveal in sharper contrast the phoniness and the tinsel of the adult world which seeks to victimize Holden, and which, in the end, finally does. Like Huck, he finds himself at the mercy of the kindly enemy. The realist's sharp perceptions of the world about him are treated either as the uncivilized remarks of an ignorant waif or—supreme irony!—as lunacy.

In addition to being comic masterpieces and superb portrayals of perplexed, sensitive adolescence, these two novels thus deal obliquely and poetically with a major theme in American life, past and present—the right of the nonconformist to assert his nonconformity, even to the point of being "handled with chain." In them, 1884 and 1951 speak to us in the idiom and accent of two youthful travelers who have earned their passports to literary immortality.

CHAPTER 3

The Character of Holden Caulfield

Holden's Language

Donald P. Costello

Donald P. Costello was one of the first to present a detailed analysis of Holden Caulfield's language. This article focuses on the vocabulary and the grammar of *The Catcher in the Rye*. Unlike many other critical articles, Costello's purpose is not to look at the images or symbols of the novel, but to explore the book as an accurate record of how teenagers in the fifties might have talked. In this excerpt, he writes that Salinger successfully created a character who maintains a distinct personality and speaks the typical prep-school teenager's language. Costello has taught at Roosevelt University and is the author of a book on George Bernard Shaw.

Even though Holden's language is authentic teenage speech, recording it was certainly not the major intention of Salinger. He was faced with the artistic task of creating an individual character, not with the linguistic task of reproducing the exact speech of teenagers in general. Yet Holden had to speak a recognizable teenage language, and at the same time had to be identifiable as an individual. This difficult task Salinger achieved by giving Holden an extremely trite and typical teenage speech, overlaid with strong personal idiosyncrasies. There are two major speech habits which are Holden's own, which are endlessly repeated throughout the book, and which are, nevertheless, typical enough of teenage speech so that Holden can be both typical and individual in his use of them. It is certainly common for teenagers to end thoughts with a loosely dangling 'and all,' just as it is common for them to add an insistent 'I really did,' 'It really was.' But Holden uses these phrases to such an overpowering degree that they become a clear part of the flavor of the book; they become, more, a part of Holden himself, and actually help to characterize him.

Reprinted from Donald P. Costello, "The Language of *The Catcher in the Rye*," *American Speech* 34 (October 1959):172–81, by permission of the author.

HOLDEN'S IDIOSYNCRATIC SPEECH PATTERNS

Holden's 'and all' and its twins, 'or something,' 'or anything,' serve no real, consistent linguistic function. They simply give a sense of looseness of expression and looseness of thought. Often they signify that Holden knows there is more that could be said about the issue at hand, but he is not going to bother going into it:

... how my parents were occupied and all before they had me.
... they're *nice* and all.
I'm not going to tell you my whole goddam autobiography
   or anything.
... splendid and clear-thinking and all.

But just as often the use of such expressions is purely arbitrary, with no discernible meaning:

... he's my *brother* and all.
... was in the Revolutionary War and all.
It was December and all.
... no gloves or anything.
... right in the pocket and all.

Donald Barr, writing in the *Commonweal*, finds this habit indicative of Holden's tendency to generalize, to find the all in the one:

> Salinger has an ear not only for idiosyncrasies of diction and syntax, but for mental processes. Holden Caulfield's phrase is 'and all'—'She looked so damn *nice*, the way she kept going around and around in her blue coat and all'—as if each experience wore a halo. His fallacy is *ab uno disce omnes;* he abstracts and generalizes wildly.

Arthur Heiserman and James Miller, in the *Western Humanities Review,* comment specifically upon Holden's second most obvious idiosyncrasy: 'In a phony world Holden feels compelled to reenforce his sincerity and truthfulness constantly with, "It really is" or "It really did."' S.N. Behrman, in the *New Yorker,* finds a double function of these 'perpetual insistences of Holden's.' Behrman thinks they 'reveal his age, even when he is thinking much older,' and, more important, 'he is so aware of the danger of slipping into phoniness himself that he has to repeat over and over "I really mean it," "It really does."' Holden uses this idiosyncrasy of insistence almost every time that he makes an affirmation.

Allied to Holden's habit of insistence is his 'if you want to know the truth.' Heiserman and Miller are able to find characterization in this habit too:

The skepticism inherent in that casual phrase, 'if you want to know the truth,' suggesting that as a matter of fact in the world of Holden Caulfield very few people do, characterizes this sixteen-year-old 'crazy mixed up kid' more sharply and vividly than pages of character 'analysis' possibly could.

Holden uses this phrase only after affirmations, just as he uses 'It really does,' but usually after the personal ones, where he is consciously being frank:

> I have no wind, if you want to know the truth.
> I don't even think that bastard had a handkerchief, if you want to know the truth.
> I'm a pacifist, if you want to know the truth.
> She had quite a lot of sex appeal, too, if you really want to know.
> I was damn near bawling, I felt so damn happy, if you want to know the truth.

These personal idiosyncrasies of Holden's speech are in keeping with general teenage language. Yet they are so much a part of Holden and of the flavor of the book that they are much of what makes Holden to be Holden. They are the most memorable feature of the book's language. Although always in character, the rest of Holden's speech is more typical than individual. The special quality of this language comes from its triteness, its lack of distinctive qualities.

HOLDEN'S CRUDE LANGUAGE

Holden's informal, schoolboy vernacular is particularly typical in its 'vulgarity' and 'obscenity.' No one familiar with prep-school speech could seriously contend that Salinger overplayed his hand in this respect. On the contrary, Holden's restraints help to characterize him as a sensitive youth who avoids the most strongly forbidden terms, and who never uses vulgarity in a self-conscious or phony way to help him be 'one of the boys.' *Fuck*, for example, is never used as a part of Holden's speech. The word appears in the novel four times, but only when Holden disapprovingly discusses its wide appearance on walls. The Divine name is used habitually by Holden only in the comparatively weak *for God's sake, God,* and *goddam.* The stronger and usually more offense *for Chrissake* or *Jesus* or *Jesus Christ* are used habitually by Ackely and Stradlater; but Holden uses them only when he feels the need for a strong expression. He almost never uses *for Chrissake* in an unemotional situation. *Goddam* is Holden's favorite adjective. This word is used with no relationship to its original meaning, or to Holden's attitude toward the word to which it is attached. It simply expresses an emotional feeling toward the object: either favorable, as in 'goddam hunting cap'; or unfavorable, as in 'ya goddam moron'; or indifferent, as in 'coming in the goddam windows.' *Damm* is used interchangeably with *goddam;* no differentiation in its meaning is detectable.

Other crude words are also often used in Holden's vocabulary. *Ass* keeps a fairly restricted meaning as a part of the human anatomy, but it is used in a variety of ways. It can refer simply to that specific part of the body ('I moved my ass a little'), or be a part of a trite expression ('freezing my ass off'; 'in a half-assed way'), or be an expletive ('Game, my ass.'). *Hell* is perhaps the most versatile word in Holden's entire vocabulary; it serves most of the meanings and constructions which Mencken lists in his *American Speech* article on 'American Profanity.' So far is Holden's use of *hell* from its original meaning that he can use the sentence 'We had a helluva time' to mean that he and Phoebe had a decidedly pleasant time downtown shopping for shoes. The most common function of *hell* is as the second part of a simile, in which a thing can be either 'hot as hell' or, strangely, 'cold as hell'; 'sad as hell' or 'playful as hell'; 'old as hell' or 'pretty as hell.' Like all of these words, *hell* has no close relationship to its original meaning.

Both *bastard* and *sonuvabitch* have also drastically changed in meaning. They no longer, of course, in Holden's vocabulary, have any connection with the accidents of birth. Unless used in a trite simile, *bastard* is a strong word, reserved for things and people Holden particularly dislikes, especially 'phonies.' *Sonuvabitch* has an even stronger meaning to Holden; he uses it only in the deepest anger. When, for example, Holden is furious with Stradlater over his treatment of Jane Gallagher, Holden repeats again and again that he 'kept calling him a moron sonuvabitch.'

The use of crude language in *The Catcher in the Rye* increases, as we should expect, when Holden is reporting schoolboy dialogue. When he is directly addressing the reader, Holden's use of such language drops off almost entirely. There is also an increase in this language when any of the characters are excited or angry. Thus, when Holden is apprehensive over Stradlater's treatment of Jane, his *goddams* increase suddenly to seven on a single page. . . .

HOLDEN'S ADAPTABLE VOCABULARY

Another aspect in which Holden's language is typical is that it shows the general American characteristic of adaptability—apparently strengthened by his teenage lack of restraint. It is very easy for Holden to turn nouns into adjectives, with the simple addition of a -*y:* 'perverty,' 'Christmasy,' 'vomity-looking,' 'whory-looking,' 'hoodlumy-looking,' 'show-offy,' 'flitty-looking,' 'dumpy-looking,' 'pimpy,' 'snobby,' 'fisty.' Like all of English, Holden's language shows a versatile combining ability: 'They gave Sally this little blue butt-twitcher of a dress to wear' and 'That magazine was some little cheerer upper.' Perhaps the most interesting aspect of the adaptability of Holden's language is his ability to use nouns as adverbs: 'She sings it very Dixieland and whore-house, and it doesn't sound at all mushy.'

As we have seen, Holden shares, in general, the trite repetitive vocabulary which is the typical lot of his age group. But as there are exceptions in his figures of speech, so are there exceptions in his vocabulary itself, in his word stock. An intelligent, well-read ('I'm quite illiterate, but I read a lot'), and educated boy, Holden possesses, and can use when he wants to, many words which are many a cut above Basic English, including 'ostracized,' 'exhibitionist,' 'unscrupulous,' 'conversationalist,' 'psychic,' 'bourgeois.' Often Holden seems to choose his words consciously, in an effort to communicate to his adult reader clearly and properly, as in such terms as 'lose my virginity,' 'relieve himself,' 'an alcoholic'; for upon occasion, he also uses the more vulgar terms 'to give someone the time,' 'to take a leak,' 'booze hound.' Much of the humor arises, in fact, from Holden's habit of writing on more than one level at the same time. Thus, we have such phrases as 'They give guys the ax quite frequently at Pencey' and 'It has a very good academic rating, Pencey.' Both sentences show a colloquial idiom with an overlay of consciously selected words.

HOLDEN'S SELF-CONSCIOUS DICTION

Such a conscious choice of words seems to indicate that Salinger, in his attempt to create a realistic character in Holden, wanted to make him aware of his speech, as, indeed, a real teenager would be when communicating to the outside world. Another piece of evidence that Holden is conscious of his speech and, more, realizes a difficulty in communication, is found in his habit of direct repetition: 'She likes me a lot. I mean she's quite fond of me,' and 'She can be very snotty sometimes. She can be quite snotty.' Sometimes the repetition is exact: 'He was a very nervous guy—I mean he was a very nervous guy,' and 'I sort of missed them. I mean I sort of missed them.' Sometimes Holden stops specifically to interpret slang terms, as when he wants to communicate the fact that Allie liked Phoebe: 'She killed Allie, too. I mean he liked her, too.'

There is still more direct evidence that Holden was conscious of his speech. Many of his comments to the reader are concerned with language. He was aware, for example, of the 'phony' quality of many words and phrases, such as 'grand,' 'prince,' 'traveling incognito,' 'little girls' room,' 'licorice stick,' and 'angels.' Holden is also conscious, of course, of the existence of 'taboo words.' He makes a point of mentioning that the girl from Seattle repeatedly asked him to 'watch your language, if you don't mind,' and that his mother told Phoebe not to say 'lousy.' When the prostitute says 'Like fun you are,' Holden comments:

> It was a funny thing to say. It sounded like a real kid. You'd think a prostitute and all would say 'Like hell you are' or 'Cut the crap' instead of 'Like fun you are.'

HOLDEN'S GRAMMAR

In grammar, too, as in vocabulary, Holden possesses a certain self-consciousness. (It is, of course, impossible to imagine a student getting through today's schools without a self-consciousness with regard to grammar rules.) Holden is, in fact, not only aware of the existence of 'grammatical errors,' but knows the social taboos that accompany them. He is disturbed by a schoolmate who is ashamed of his parents' grammar, and he reports that his former teacher, Mr. Antolini, warned him about picking up 'just enough education to hate people who say, "It's a secret between he and I."'

Holden is a typical enough teenager to violate the grammar rules, even though he knows of their social importance. His most common rule violation is the misuse of *lie* and *lay*, but he also is careless about relative pronouns ('about a traffic cop that falls in love'), the double negative ('I hardly didn't even know I was doing it'), the perfect tenses ('I'd woke him up'), extra words ('like as if all you ever did at

Pency was play polo all the time'), pronoun number ('it's pretty disgusting to watch somebody picking their nose'), and pronoun position ('I and this friend of mine, Mal Brossard'). More remarkable, however, than the instances of grammar rule violations is Holden's relative 'correctness.' Holden is always intelligible, and is even 'correct' in many usually difficult constructions. Grammatically speaking, Holden's language seems to point up the fact that English was the only subject in which he was not failing. It is interesting to note how much more 'correct' Holden's speech is than that of Huck Finn. But then Holden is educated, and since the time of Huck there had been sixty-seven years of authoritarian schoolmarms working on the likes of Holden. He has, in fact, been overtaught, so that he uses many 'hyper' forms:

> I used to play tennis with he and Mrs. Antolini quite
> frequently.
> She'd give Allie or I a push.
> I and Allie used to take her to the park with us.
> I think I probably woke he and his wife up.

. . . The language of *The Catcher in the Rye* is, as we have seen, an authentic artistic rendering of a type of informal, colloquial, teenage American spoken speech. It is strongly typical and trite, yet often somewhat individual; it is crude and slangy and imprecise, imitative yet occasionally imaginative, and affected toward standardization by the strong efforts of schools. But authentic and interesting as this language may be, it must be remembered that it exists, in *The Catcher in the Rye,* as only one part of an artistic achievement. The language was not written for itself, but as a part of a greater whole. Like the great Twain work with which it is often compared, a study of *The Catcher in the Rye* repays both the linguist and the literary critic; for as one critic has said, 'In them, 1884 and 1951 speak to us in the idiom and accent of two youthful travelers who have earned their passports to literary immortality.'

Holden Caulfield: An Unreliable Narrator

Susan K. Mitchell

The influential critic Roland Barthes made the distinction between viewing the world as a reader or as a writer. Barthes says that whereas readers only encounter a text once, writers encounter a text a number of times. He claims that this writerly way of seeing allows us to explore one story in a deeper, more fulfilling way. Literary critic Susan K. Mitchell adopts this idea and applies it to *The Catcher in the Rye*. She argues that we cannot trust Holden's narration because he refuses to look beyond the surface level of his world (i.e., he sees it "readerly"). Because Holden is not a reliable narrator, the portraits he draws of his family are not entirely accurate. Susan Mitchell teaches at Texas Tech University.

In [*The Catcher in the Rye*], Holden has analyzed his family as a representative slice of society and has concluded that adult society is phony and corrupt. But can we really trust his observations of his family after he has told us that he lies? Is he not, like the Cretan who declared that all Cretans were liars, a person declaring that all people are phony? If everyone is phony, then he is phony, too! Although Holden has claimed that he is a liar, he does not always realize whether he is lying or telling the truth. The distinctions between truth and falsehood become blurred as he often adds the phrase "to tell you the truth" onto whatever he is saying. But does this catchphrase ensure that his words are any more truthful? This unambiguous rhetorical statement is restated in an even more paradoxical way when Holden tells Sally that he loves her and then comments to the reader, "It was a lie, of course, but the thing is, I *meant* it when I said it." Again we are forced to read the work, as Paul de Man sug-

Reprinted from Susan K. Mitchell, "'To Tell You the Truth . . . ,'" *CLA Journal* 36 (1992):145–56, by permission of the College Language Association.

gests, [in "Semiology and Rhetoric," *Contemporary Literary Criticism,* ed. Robert Con Davis (New York: Longman, 1986), p. 474] in "two entirely coherent but entirely incompatible" ways. Is he lying, or does he "mean" it? First we may claim that Holden is telling the truth: he is a liar, people are phony, society is corrupt. Or we may claim that Holden is lying: he is truthful, people are genuine, and society is untainted.

There are obvious problems with both sides of this paradox. Can Holden, people, and society be entirely unchanging—always lying, always corrupt, always phony? Or are there internal forces within each that cause them to change (un)willingly? Holden would argue that each is unchanging, labeled forever. In fact, this is how he presents his information to us. He may go out with Sally, but he does not harbor any hope that she will cast off her phoniness. He may loan Stradlater his coat, but he still believes Stradlater is a phony.

ROLAND BARTHES'S THEORY OF PERCEIVING REALITY

Because we view all of the events in the book through the eyes of one narrator, our observations are necessarily biased. Holden is an unreliable narrator not only because he is a self-proclaimed liar but also because he perceives reality in a simplistic way. In his work *S/Z*, Roland Barthes outlines two ways of perceiving reality: *readerly* and *writerly.* Barthes explains these ideas in terms of reading books. He claims that the only way to read a different story is to reread the same book. By rereading, a person can learn how this book differs from itself rather than how it differs from other books. When a reader rereads a work, he is perceiving writerly. When a reader refuses to reread, Barthes maintains that he is condemned to "read the same story everywhere." Holden refuses to reread as he perceives reality readerly, seeing only the surface differences between people, not the underlying differences within each person. To perceive a person readerly would be to perceive in terms of overt, easily distinguishable differences.

HOLDEN SEES THE SAME STORY EVERYWHERE

Because Holden avoids investigating deeply, he sees the same story everywhere. Everyone is phony, he insists. But can we honestly believe him? Is he telling the truth? Even so, he is not passing on false or limited information since he has not gone to the trouble to read one story well. To approach accuracy, Holden would have to perceive a person writerly, to judge the fragmentation, the differences within the person, the covert, often contradictory intentions that war within and cause overt actions. We can draw conclusions only from the data which Holden perceives and selects to reveal to us (and he does select carefully as when he refuses to discuss his childhood or his parents); hence, we must be astute readers indeed lest we miss the multidimensionality of the characters that he develops. His readerly perception creates blinkers for the reader.

HOLDEN'S VIEW OF HIS PARENTS

Throughout the novel, Holden tries to lull us into accepting his view of surrounding life as he makes statements that seem to make sense, but which, upon closer inspection, do not bear up to a writerly view. This simplistic mode of perception is revealed particularly through his description of his family. First of all, the Caulfield parents are described in such a way as to cause the blinkered reader to view them uncompromisingly as irresponsible, alienated, skittish parents. For example, the parents are off at work away from their children, who are scattered throughout the country: D.B. in Hollywood, Allie dead, Phoebe at home, and Holden at Pencey Prep. Mr. and Mrs. Caulfield seem to be isolated characters. The reader never meets Mr. Caulfield and only hears Mrs. Caulfield when Holden is hiding in Phoebe's room. Holden will not tell much about his parents beyond his veiled opinion that they both are phony hypocrites. The reader is not even told their first names. From the beginning we are led to believe that they are hypersensitive about Holden's revealing their personal life because they want to protect their created image of conformed perfection. Because Mrs. Caulfield is a nervous woman who has smoked compulsively ever since Allie's death, Holden avoids confrontation about his being kicked out of Pencey Prep. He therefore hides from her as he stays in a hotel or in Mr. Antolini's apartment. Each of these examples appears to show that Mrs. Caulfield does not really communicate with her children. On the other hand, Mr. Caulfield is a lawyer. Holden makes no bones about his opinion of lawyers: they "make a lot of dough and play golf and play bridge and buy cars and drink Martinis and look like a hot-shot" and are phony but can't know it.

Holden's warped view of his parents denigrates them without even considering that the Caulfields may be blameless. Can we really trust Holden's view of his parents? Isn't he unethically stacking the deck so that we are prohibited from obtaining an objective view of them? We are given so few facts and scenes to describe them that we have trouble refuting Holden, except that we know he is holding something back from us. No couple could merit such a denunciation from a son. If what he has revealed about the Caulfields is true, carefully selected though the information may be, can we blame them for their anger, hysteria, and desire for privacy? These would be logical reactions if an offspring were so apathetic as to be kicked out of several reputable schools and then became anxious to write a book about his family while recovering from insanity. And what is wrong about working hard to support children, to enable them to have the best education possible? What exactly is phony about being a lawyer? Even though Holden's vagueness works well for him, making his parents appear base, mercenary, isolated, distant, and careless, it denies any redeeming qualities that would upset Holden's persuasive thesis that adult society is corrupt....

HOLDEN PERCEIVES READERLY

Naturally, Holden is the only character shown to be heroically struggling with exactly how to relate to society. He is locked into a self that desires to be genuine but finds no way to return to the pastoral ideal. He believes that he is holed in, trapped by the games of phoniness that society requires its citizens to play. He tries to escape this trap by flunking out of school and by searching for a quiet retreat, only to discover that there is no pure retreat on earth—log cabins are distant and lonely, deserted museum rooms are corrupted with permanent obscenities, private hotel rooms lure prostitutes and pimps. Frustrated by the readerly evidence which he has gathered to support his thesis, Holden is himself fragmented and ravaged by the warring forces within him. For instance, within Holden, the desire to reject others conflicts with the desire to be accepted by others; he doesn't want to lend Stradlater his coat, but his overt actions belie this covert, warring want; he despises Ackely, but he invites him to see a movie; he hates movies, believing them to foster phoniness in society, but during the three days of the book he sees or talks about several; he craves truth, but he tells blatant lies. Despite his own inherent writerliness or differences within, Holden still perceives only readerly. He views himself as a liar, but he refuses to acknowledge that this means that he is phony, too. In fact, Holden views writerliness as a kind of individual fragmentation or disorientation of the individual, a symbol, in his mind, of a corrupt society.

HOLDEN BECOMES AWARE OF HIS WRITERLINESS

When Holden does become aware of his own writerliness, he goes over the brink into insanity. Throughout the work, he has become more and more frustrated in his awkward attempts to establish genuine friendships and to find quiet retreats. He even tries to restore purity in the schools by erasing obscenities so that children can be preserved from corruption for as long as possible. However, he is forced to confront his own writerly corruption when he is in the museum and sees an obscenity written in red beneath a glass plate. He is not the savior of children; he is not called to be the catcher in the rye. He is just a corrupt human being himself, a being who uses obscenities freely in his own casual conversation. Now that he has acknowledged his own writerliness, purged (symbolically through diarrhea) his traditional method of readerly perception, and symbolically fallen to show that he has accepted his writerly nature, he begins to see the world in a writerly manner. He is astonished and delighted to find that the carousel is the same after all these years:

> We kept getting closer and closer to the carousel and you could start to hear that nutty music it always plays. It was playing "Oh, Marie!" It played that same song about fifty years ago when *I* was a little kid. That's one nice thing about carousels, they always play the same songs.

However, now that his eyes are opened, he can see a new richness within the carousel that he has seen many times before. Now it teaches him that children will try to grab the gold ring and he must let them: "If they fall off, they fall off, but it's bad if you say anything to them."

Will Holden slip back into his readerliness? One indication that he will not is that he has decided to write about his own experiences, to analyze himself in terms of the world around him. He is seeking perhaps for the first time to reread his own story and understand it as different from all other stories.

The Catcher in the Rye Should Not Be Reduced to a Novel About Male Adolescence

Mary Suzanne Schriber

In this excerpt, feminist critic Mary Suzanne Schriber examines how most critical articles about *Catcher* tend to generalize the male character Holden as typical of all adolescents. Schriber argues that this thinking necessarily excludes women from the dialogue. Thus, the male critic sees himself in Holden and assumes the rest of America does as well. Schriber believes that traditional literary criticism endorses the image of all humanity as strictly male. This androcentric (or male-centered) point of view taints the criticism to date on *Catcher* and therefore *Catcher*'s place in the literary canon is compromised. Schriber is distinguished professor of English at Northern Illinois University. She is the author of *Gender and the Writer's Imagination* and the editor of *Telling Tales: Selected Writings of Nineteenth-Century Women Abroad.*

The essential ingredient in the phenomenal success and the critical reception of *The Catcher in the Rye is* the propensity of critics to identify with Salinger's protagonist. Holden Caulfield, c'est moi. Falling in love with him as with their very selves, they fall in love with the novel as well. The criticism indicates that they see in Holden, and in themselves through his agency, an incarnation of their youth. Having identified with Holden, critics then engage in a procedure that magnifies him. Undeterred by and apparently oblivious to Holden's gender (and his social and economic class as well), they first assume maleness as the norm. Next, they

Reprinted from Mary Suzanne Schriber, "Holden Caulfield, C'est Moi," in *Critical Essays on Salinger's "The Catcher in the Rye,"* edited by Joel Salzburg (Boston: G.K. Hall, 1990), by permission of the author.

are reinforced in this assumption by male-identified and gender-inflected theories of American literature, regnant for thirty years, within which more than a generation of readers has been taught to situate American novels. Developed by scholars who have themselves conflated the human and the male, these theories guide critics as they construe and construct the meaning of *Catcher* and its place in American literary history. They enable critics to find in Salinger's novel that which has been defined as archetypally American and thus classic, a literary work of timeless and universal significance. . . .

While identifying with Holden in their manhood as well as in their youth, critics have failed "to consider gender a relevant factor in either the configuration of identity or the institution of literature itself."[1] This occurs even when the critic is less than fond of the novel but perceives it nonetheless, like Ernest Jones, as "a case history of all of us," apparently defining "us" as male.[2] Presuming that the male is synonymous with the human, critics absorb the female into the male, particularly in their treatment of Holden and sexuality. Brian Way, for example, writes that in New York Holden embarks "on a dream" that is "universally adolescent": "the offer of unbelievable possibilities of sexual adventure and satisfaction." Way does not perceive this as a male's sense of adventure but, rather, he takes it to be normative; he praises Salinger for going "straight to the fundamental biological situation. [Salinger] sees that all the contradictions, agonies, and exaltations of adolescence stem from the central fact: that the adolescent has newly gained the physical potentialities for sexual experience but has not learnt to integrate them either within himself or in any consistent relation to the demands of society."[3] The notion of a "fundamental biological situation" overlooks the differential development, place, and manifestations of sexuality for males and females in the adolescent years. . . .

A Look at Kaplan's Essay

The criticism of *The Catcher in the Rye* shows the degree to which literary theory is responsible for the attribution of

---

1. Sidonie Smith, *A Poetics of Women's Autobiography* (Bloomington: Indiana University Press, 1987), 15.   2. Ernest Jones, "Case History of All of Us," *Nation*, 1 September 1951, 176.   3. Brian Way, "'Franny and Zooey' and J.D. Salinger," *New Left Review*, May–June 1962; reprinted as "A Tight Three-Movement Structure" in *Studies*, 194, 196.

global significance to the tale of a WASP preppy male youth. Critics clearly impose on or find in (as the case may be) Holden Caulfield and his adventures the definitions of essential "Americanness" that characterize the work of Lionel Trilling . . . and others. The trend began as early as 1956, in Charles Kaplan's essay entitled "Holden and Huck: The Odysseys of Youth." As the title forewarns us, Huck and Holden are about to become "youth" itself, apparently entirely male, as it sets off, in Kaplan's words, on "an adventure story in the age-old pattern of a young lad making his way in a not particularly friendly adult world." Having immasculated "youth," it is easy to immasculate "adolescence" as well, as Kaplan proceeds to do: "In addition to being comic masterpieces and superb portrayals of perplexed, sensitive adolescence, these two novels thus deal obliquely and poetically with a major theme in American life, past and present—the right of the nonconformist to assert his nonconformity, even to the point of being 'handled with a chain.' In them, 1884 and 1951 speak to us in the idiom and accent of two youthful travelers who have earned their passports to literary immortality."[4] Notice how that which is associated with the male, in Kaplan's rhetoric, has progressively absorbed everything in its path. "Youth" and "adolescence" are first implicitly masculinized. Next, that which has been masculinized is expanded into a theme in the whole of "American life," and even immortalized by being projected into both "past and present." Then this all-consuming male, encompassing "youth" and "adolescence" and "America . . . past and present" draws the "nonconformist" into its system. The coup de grace, however, the most chilling manifestation of the insidious power of this androcentric habit over the perceiving mind—insidious because it remains invisible while selecting that which will become visible—occurs in the quote: "handled with a chain."

Kaplan's relentlessly immasculating rhetoric first does its work on "nonconformist" and then, ironically, on Emily Dickinson's "Much Madness Is Divinest Sense." Having assimilated everything into the male, Kaplan's rhetoric then either contradicts the equation of "nonconformist" with the male or manages to immasculate none other than Emily

4. Charles Kaplan, "Holden and Huck: The Odysseys of Youth," *College English* 18 (November 1956); reprinted in *Studies,* 31, 37–38.

Dickinson. Theories of American literature that implicitly govern Kaplan's reading can be credited with this, theories that conflate American and male experience and proceed to blind the critic even to so strong a female presence as that of Emily Dickinson and to the implicit contradictions in his own critical text. . . .

Thus the popularity and the ascription of broad significance and exceptional literary importance to *The Catcher in the Rye* can be traced to nurturing arrangements, to assumptions that the male is the normative, and to androcentric theories of American literature in which American fiction is routinely framed and taught. Yet a qualification is in order here. The reading experience of many of us, female as well as male (and rural as well as urban, Catholic and Jewish as well as WASP), is articulated in many of the claims made for Salinger's novel. Reader response, and not just the rhetoric of critics, suggests that *Catcher* is a fiction that *does* capture and express recognizable parts of adolescence. Does Salinger's novel more than "seemingly" escape, somehow, the confines of gender to touch broad if not universal human sensibilities? Perhaps the response to this novel should warn us that "concentrating on gender difference can lead us to slight the affinity of women and men . . . the common ground shared by all humans."[5] Moreover, if the criticism of *Catcher* manages by and large to articulate the intuitions of many readers of both genders, how can that criticism fairly be labeled androcentric and accused of a masculinist imperialism that mistakes part of human experience for the whole? Or on the other hand, have we been duped into finding ourselves in Salinger's novel by the androcentric logic in which we are schooled? Is the reading of *Catcher* an instance in which "androcentricity *may* be a sufficient condition for the process of immasculation"?[6]

CATCHER CRITICISM GUILTY OF ANDROCENTRICITY

Catcher criticism is guilty of androcentricity as charged because it fails to be self-reflexive. It remains oblivious to the possibility of a female perspective; it fails to problematize the male (and the urban and the WASP); it remains shackled to "false and damaging 'universals' that saddle the major

5. Patrocinio Schweickart and Elizabeth Flynn, *Gender and Reading*, xxix.   6. Patrocinio Schweickart, "Reading Ourselves: Toward a Feminist Theory of Reading," in *Gender and Reading*, 42.

intellectual discourses."[7] It does not declare its assumptions and explain where *Catcher* gets "its power to draw us into its designs," whether from an appeal to authentic desires for liberation and maturity or sheer complicity in our androcentric conditioning.[8] *Catcher* criticism arrogantly assumes that the male includes, unproblematically and unquestionably, the female, the adolescent, and the nation itself, as if this were a given in the natural order of things, requiring no comment and no explanation. Having spoken to and for an exceptionally large audience for four decades, *The Catcher in the Rye* perhaps legitimately deserves its popularity and its designation as a "classic." The critical case for *Catcher*, however, remains to be made. Contrary to the silences and assertions of Salinger criticism to date, an adolescent male WASP is not automatically nature's designated spokesperson for us all.

---

7. Schweickart and Flynn, *Gender and Reading*, xxix.   8. Schweickart, "Reading Ourselves," in *Gender and Reading*, 42–43.

CHAPTER 4

The Catcher in the Rye: A Critical Evaluation

The Catcher in the Rye Should Not Be Censored

Edward P.J. Corbett

The Catcher in the Rye has been one of the most frequently banned books in America in the past few
decades. High school libraries and classrooms have
removed the book because of objections to its content and language. Ten years after the novel's publication in 1951, Edward P.J. Corbett, a Jesuit priest
and teacher, wrote this defense of the novel, taking
on the specific charges of the critics. He claims that
although the detractors have some justification for
their complaints, the novel as a whole is neither immoral nor corrupting. Corbett has taught at
Creighton University and is a frequent contributor to
America. He also writes on rhetoric and composition.

About six years ago [1955], at a Modern Language Association convention, a group of professors were discussing job
openings, as is their wont at such gatherings. One of the
teachers mentioned an offer he had had from a West Coast
college. A pipe-smoker in the group blurted out: "For
heaven's sake, stay away from *that* place. They recently fired
a man for requiring his freshman students to read *The
Catcher in the Rye.*"

That firing may have been the earliest instance of a
teacher getting into serious trouble over J.D. Salinger's book.
Since that time, reports of irate protests from school boards,
principals, librarians and parents have multiplied. The most
publicized recent stir about the book was the reprimand that
Mrs. Beatrice Levin received from her principal for introducing *The Catcher in the Rye* to her 16-year-old students at
Edison High School in Tulsa, Okla. Scores of subsequent letters to the editor revealed other bans on the book in schools

Reprinted from Edward P.J. Corbett, "Raise High the Barriers, Censors," *America* 104
(January 14, 1961):441–44, by permission of the author.

and libraries. Curiously enough, the same kind of censure was once visited upon the book to which *The Catcher in the Rye* has most often been compared—Mark Twain's *Huckleberry Finn.*

Adult attempts to keep *The Catcher in the Rye* out of the hands of young people will undoubtedly increase, for it is the one novel that young people of postwar generation have been reading and discussing avidly. . . .

To the many people who have come to love the book and its hero, Holden Caulfield, all this controversy is puzzling and disturbing. They regard even the suggestion that the book needs defending as sacrilegious—almost as though they were being asked to vindicate the Constitution. Although their feelings of outrage are understandable, I feel that in view of the vast and continuing popularity of the book the objections should be confronted and appraised. My arguments in defense of *The Catcher in the Rye* are the common ones, quite familiar to those acquainted with other controversies about "forbidden" books.

THE LANGUAGE OF THE BOOK IS CRUDE, PROFANE, OBSCENE

This is the objection most frequently cited when the book has been banned. From one point of view, this objection is the easiest to answer; from another point of view, it is the hardest to answer.

Considered in isolation, the language *is* crude and profane. It would be difficult to argue, however, that such language is unfamiliar to our young people or that it is rougher than the language they are accustomed to hear in the streets among their acquaintances, But there is no question about it, a vulgar expression seen in print is much more shocking than one that is spoken. Lewd scribblings on sidewalks or on the walls of rest-rooms catch our attention and unsettle our sensibilities; and they become most shocking when they are seen in the sanctity of the printed page. Traditionally, novelists have been keenly aware of the shock value of printed profanities. Stephen Leacock has a delightful essay in which he reviews the many circumlocutions and typographical devices that novelists since the 18th century have employed to avoid the use of shocking expressions.

Granting the shock potential of such language, especially to youngsters, must we also grant it a corrupting influence? To deny that words can shape our attitudes and influence our actions would be to deny the rhetorical power of language. But to maintain that four-letter words of themselves are obscene and can corrupt is another matter. Interestingly enough, most reports about the banning of this novel have told that some principal or librarian or parent hastily paged through the book and spotted several four-letter words. That was evidence enough; the book must go. It is natural, although not always prudent, for adults to want to protect the young from shock. And this concern may be sufficient justification for adults wanting to keep the book out of the hands of grade-school children or the more immature high school students. But one of the unfortunate results of banning the book for this reason is that the very action of banning creates the impression that the book is nasty and highly corrosive of morals.

As has happened in many censorship actions in the past, parts are judged in isolation from the whole. The soundest defense that can be advanced for the language of this novel is a defense based on the art of the novel. Such a defense could be stated like this: Given the point of view from which the novel is told, and given the kind of character that figures as the hero, no other language was possible. The integrity of the novel demanded such language.

But even when readers have been willing to concede that the bold language is a necessary part of the novel, they have expressed doubts about the authenticity of Holden's language. Teen-age girls, I find, are especially skeptical about the authenticity of the language. "Prep-school boys just don't talk like that," they say. It is a tribute, perhaps, to the gentlemanliness of adolescent boys that when they are in the company of girls they temper their language. But, whatever the girls may think, prep-school boys do on occasion talk as Holden talks. As a matter of fact, Holden's patois is remarkably restrained in comparison with the blue-streak vernacular of his real-life counterparts. Holden's profanity becomes most pronounced in moments of emotional tension; at other times his language is notably tempered—slangy, ungrammatical, rambling, yes, but almost boyishly pure. Donald P. Costello, who made a study of the language of *The Catcher in the Rye* for the journal *American Speech* (October 1959), concluded that Salinger had given "an accurate rendering of the informal speech of an intelligent, educated, Northeastern American adolescent." "No one familiar with prep school speech," Costello goes on to say, "could seriously contend that Salinger overplayed his hand in this respect."

Holden's swearing is so habitual, so unintentional, so ritualistic that it takes on a quality of innocence. Holden is characterized by a desperate bravado; he is constantly seeking to appear older than he really is. Despite that trait, however, Holden's profanity does not stem from the same motivation that prompts other adolescents to swear—the urge to seem "one of the boys." His profanity is so much ingrained by habit into the fabric of his speech that he is wholly unaware of how rough his language is. Twice his little sister Phoebe reminds him to stop swearing so much. Holden doesn't even pause to apologize for his language; he doesn't even advert to the fact that his sister has reprimanded him. And it is not because he has become callous, for this is the same boy who flew into a rage when he saw the obscenity scribbled on a wall where it might be seen by little children.

SOME OF THE EPISODES IN THE BOOK ARE SCANDALOUS

The episode commonly cited as being unfit for adolescents to read is the one about the prostitute in the hotel room. A case could be made out for the view that young people should not be exposed to such descriptions. It would be much the same case that one makes out in support of the view that children of a certain age should not be allowed to play with matches. But a convincing case cannot be, and never has been, made out for the view that vice should never be portrayed in a novel.

One shouldn't have to remind readers of what Cardinal Newman once said, that we cannot have a sinless literature about a sinful people. That reminder, however, has to be made whenever a censorship controversy comes up. The proper distinction in this matter is that no novel is immoral merely because vice is represented in it. Immorality creeps in as a result of the author's attitude toward the vice he is portraying and his manner of rendering the scene.

Let us consider the scene in question according to this norm in order to test the validity of the charge that it is scandalous. First of all, neither the novelist nor his character regards the assignation with the prostitute as proper or even as morally indifferent. The word *sin* is not part of Holden's vocabulary, but throughout the episode Holden is acutely aware that the situation in which he finds himself is producing an uncomfortable tension, a tormenting conflict, within him. And that vague awareness of disturbance, of something being "wrong," even if the character doesn't assign the label "sin" to it, is enough to preserve the moral tone of the scene in question.

Some readers seem to forget, too, that Holden didn't seek this encounter with the prostitute. He was trapped into it; he was a victim, again, of his own bravado. "It was against my principles and all," he says, "but I was feeling so depressed I didn't even *think.*" Nor does he go through with the act. Embarrassment, nervousness, inexperience—all play a part in his rejection of the girl. But what influences his decision most, without his being aware of it, is his pity for the girl. That emotion is triggered by the sight of her green dress. It is that pity which introduces a moral note into Holden's choice. Nor does Salinger render this scene with the kind of explicit, erotic detail that satisfies the pruriency of readers who take a lickerish delight in pornography. All of the scenes about sexual matters are tastefully, even beautifully, treated. Is it any wonder that devotees of the novel are shocked by the suggestion that some of the scenes are scandalous?

HOLDEN, CONSTANTLY PROTESTING AGAINST PHONINESS, IS A PHONY HIMSELF

With this objection we move close to a charge against the novel that is damaging because it is based on sounder premises than the other two objections. No doubt about it, Salinger likes this boy, and he wants his readers to like the boy, too. If it could be shown that Salinger, despite his intentions, failed to create a sympathetic character, all the current fuss about the novel would be rendered superfluous, because the novel would eventually fall of its own dead weight.

Holden uses the word *phony* or some derivative of it at least 44 times. *Phoniness* is the generic term that Holden uses to cover all manifestations of cant, hypocrisy and speciosity. He is genuinely disturbed by such manifestations, so much so that, to use his own forthright term, he wants to "puke." The reason why he finds the nuns, his sister Phoebe and children in general so refreshing is that they are free of this phoniness.

But, as a number of people charge, Holden is himself a phony. He is an inveterate liar; he frequently masquerades as someone he is not; he fulminates against foibles of which he himself is guilty; he frequently vents his spleen about his friends, despite the fact that he seems to be advocating the need for charity. Maxwell Geismar puts this objection most pointedly when he says: "*The Catcher in the Rye* protests, to be sure, against both the academic and social conformity of its period. But what does it argue *for?*" Because of this inconsistency between what Holden wants other people to be and what he is himself, many readers find the boy a far from sympathetic character and declare that he is no model for our young people to emulate.

These readers have accurately described what Holden *does*, but they miss the point about what he *is*. Holden is the classic portrait of "the crazy, mixed-up kid," but with this significant difference: there is about him a solid substratum of goodness, genuineness and sensitivity. It is just this conflict between the surface and the substratum that makes the reading of the novel such a fascinating, pathetic and intensely moral experience. Because Holden is more intelli-

---

A CASE OF CENSORSHIP

In 1989 the Boron, California, school board voted to remove The Catcher in the Rye *from the school's supplemental reading list because they felt it was obscene. The teacher who assigned the book, Mrs. Keller-Gage, likens the small-town censors to the novel's main character, Holden Caulfield: Both are trying unsuccessfully to protect children from losing their innocence.*

BORON, Calif., Aug. 30—If a group of local parents had let her speak to them before "The Catcher in the Rye" was banned from her high school classroom, Shelley Keller-Gage says she would have told them she believes it is a highly moral book that deals with the kinds of difficulties their own children are facing.

But she was asked not to speak, and a group of angry parents, led by a woman who says she has not—and never would—read such a book, persuaded the school board to ban it this month from the Boron High School supplementary reading list.

"Unfortunately, what happened is not at all unusual," said Anne Levinson, assistant director of the Office of Intellectual Freedom in Chicago. "Censorship is still very much with us. As a matter of fact, I think 'The Catcher in the Rye' is a perennial No. 1 on the censorship hit list."

Ms. Levinson said J.D. Salinger's 1951 novel about a troubled

gent and more sensitive than his confreres, he has arrived prematurely at the agonizing transition between adolescence and adulthood. He is precocious but badly seasoned. An affectionate boy, yearning for love and moorings, he has been cut off during most of his teen-age years from the haven of his family. Whatever religious training he has been exposed to has failed to touch him or served to confuse him. Accordingly, he is a young man adrift in an adult world that buffets and bewilders him.

The most salient mark of Holden's immaturity is his inability to discriminate. His values are sound enough, but he views everything out of proportion. Most of the manners and mores that Holden observes and scorns are not as monstrous as Holden makes them out to be. His very style of speech, with its extraordinary propensity for hyperbole, is evidence of this lack of a sense of proportion. Because he will not discriminate, he is moving dangerously close to that most tragic of all states, negation. His sister Phoebe tells him

---

teen-ager named Holden Caulfield seems to have a narrow lead over John Steinbeck's "Of Mice and Men" and "Grapes of Wrath" in arousing the objections of communities or special-interest groups around the country that are increasingly moving to ban books.

On Wednesday, People for the American Way, a group that opposes censorship, issued a report listing 172 incidents in 42 states of attempted or successful censorship in schools in the last year, illustrating what the group's president, Arthur Kropp, called "an unreasonable undercurrent of fear about the so-called 'dangers' of public school instruction."

The report, the group's seventh annual censorship roundup, said efforts to restrict books and curriculums from classrooms and school libraries were on the rise nationwide, with nearly half of them succeeding.

The school board's 4-to-1 vote has aroused this small sun-baked town of 4,000 at the edge of the Mojave Desert, and when Mrs. Keller-Gage, a 35-year-old Boron native, goes out she said she hears a buzzing of, "That's her. There she goes."

Although "The Catcher in the Rye" is now banned from Boron's classrooms, it has gained a new readership among townspeople, and Helen Nelson, the local librarian, has a waiting list of 15 people for the book that she says has been sitting on the shelf all these years pretty much unnoticed.

Seth Mydans, *New York Times*, September 3, 1989.

"You don't like *any*thing that's happening." Holden's reaction to this charge gives the first glimmer of hope that he may seek the self-knowledge which can save him.

Holden must get to know himself. As Mr. Antolini, his former teacher, tells him: "You're going to have to find out where you want to go." But Holden needs most of all to develop a sense of humor. One of the most startling paradoxes about this book is that although it is immensely funny, there is not an ounce of humor in Holden himself. With the development of a sense of humor will come the maturity that can straighten him out. He will begin to see himself as others see him.

The lovely little scene near the end of the book in which Phoebe is going around and around on the carousel can be regarded as an objective correlative of Holden's condition at the end of his ordeal by disillusionment. Up to this point, Holden has pursued his odyssey in a more or less straight line; but in the end, in his confusion and heartsickness, he is swirling around in a dizzying maelstrom. In the final chapter, however, it would appear that Holden has had his salutary epiphany. "I sort of *miss* everybody I told about," he says. Here is the beginning of wisdom. The reader is left with the feeling that Holden, because his values are fundamentally sound, will turn out all right.

I suspect that adults who object to Holden on the grounds of his apparent phoniness are betraying their own uneasiness. Holden is not like the adolescents in the magazine ads—the smiling, crew-cut, loafer-shod teen-agers wrapped up in the cocoon of suburban togetherness. He makes the adults of my generation uncomfortable because he exposes so much of what is meretricious in our way of life.

THE DANGER OF DEFENDING *CATCHER*

In defending *The Catcher in the Rye*, one is liable to the danger of exaggerating J.D. Salinger's achievement and potential. As George Steiner has warned in the *Nation* (Nov. 14, 1959), there is a vigorous "Salinger industry" under way now, which could put Salinger's work badly out of focus. Judged in the company of other post-war fiction, *The Catcher in the Rye* is an extraordinary novel. His earlier short stories, especially "For Esmé—with Love and Squalor," are truly distinguished. But the last two long, diffuse stories to appear in the *New Yorker*, "Zooey" and "Seymour," have been something of a disappointment. They are fascinating as experiments with the short-story form, but they strike me as being an accumulation of finger exercises rather than the finished symphony. If we admirers of Salinger can keep our heads about us, maybe we can make it possible for Salinger to build on the promise of his earlier work.

In the meantime, some concession must be made, I suppose, to the vigilantes who want to keep *The Catcher in the Rye* out of the hands of the very young. Future controversy will probably center on just what age an adolescent must be before he is ready for this book. That may prove to be a futile dispute. But I would hope that any decisions about the book would be influenced by the consideration, not that this is an immoral, corrupting book—for it is certainly not—but that it is a subtle, sophisticated novel that requires an experienced, mature reader. Above all, let the self-appointed censors *read* the novel before they raise the barriers.

An Attack on *Catcher*

Lawrence Jay Dessner

Not all critics like Holden Caulfield. In this attack on the novel, Lawrence Jay Dessner claims that Salinger creates a character who is the essence of our most immature selves and asks readers to admire him. Dessner does not let his fellow literary critics off the hook; they too share in some of the blame for praising the book and increasing its popularity. Dessner writes that some critics' comparisons of *The Catcher in the Rye* to great works of literature by authors such as Mark Twain or Fyodor Dostoyevsky is an embarrassment. Dessner is professor of English at the University of Toledo. He publishes poetry and is the author of *How to Write a Poem.*

In the ten years after its publication in July of 1951 *The Catcher in the Rye* sold over one and one-half million copies. It was adopted as a text in some 300 American colleges and universities, and in countless secondary schools. A great deal of what is called "research" was published on it. In dismay, George Steiner did what he could to stem the flood. He disparaged what he named "The Salinger Industry," called Holden Caulfield "the young lout," and bemoaned comparisons of him with "Alyosha Karamazov, Aeneas, Ulysses, Gatsby, Ishmael, Hans Castorp, and Dostoevsky's Idiot." Steiner added, mischievously but with anger too, that these comparisons "were always rather to [Caulfield's] own advantage." He spoke of the novel's flattery of the ignorant and of ignorance itself, and of its "shoddy . . . half-culture," and he tried to discover why it is that "literary criticism [is] so determined to get [things] out of proportion." Why, this "gross devaluation of standards.". . .

The Catcher in the Rye has been most often compared to Mark Twain's *Adventures of Huckleberry Finn,* compared, that is, in terms of form, characters, plot, humor and all this

Reprinted from Lawrence Jay Dessner, "The Salinger Story; or, Have It Your Way," in *Seasoned* Authors *for a New Season: The Search for Standards in Popular Writing,* edited by Louis Filler (Bowling Green, OH: Bowling Green University Popular Press, 1980), by permission of the publisher.

so assiduously that comparison of value, that comparison which would justify making all the others, is ignored, value tacitly assumed. The novels are "akin also in ethical-social import." "Each book," another critic continues, "is a devastating criticism of American society and voices a morality of love and humanity." Steiner grits his teeth; Mark Twain turns over yet again in his grave. And I cannot forbear asking about that "morality of love and humanity." Is there some other kind? Is there a morality of love but not of humanity, or of humanity and not of love? Is this morality "voiced" by Salinger, by Holden? Have we been reading the same book? May one professor turn another one over on his knee and deliver corporal punishment? Is the view of American society which Salinger's novel devastatingly criticizes a fair and accurate view of that society? Is Pencey Prep more than an ill-tempered caricature of some lesser Andover? Is there, in all of *The Catcher in the Rye,* any reference to the historical or political or economic conditions of its moment? Well, I guess there must be, because one of the more eminent commentators on modern literature, after quoting Thoreau and breathlessly wondering "what is the sound of one hand clapping," assures us that "Salinger proves . . . to be seriously engaged by a current and a traditional aspect of reality in America." Wow! Both a current *and* a traditional aspect of reality. Once upon a time, Robert Browning sent a copy of his famously obscure long poem, *The Ring and the Book,* to a literary friend who had been seriously ill. "It's my mind," his friend cried out from his sickbed. "My strength is coming back but my mind is going. I can't understand the English language any more."

Since the earlier days of Salinger's prominence, criticism has followed the method of praise by association and implication. Some of the more imaginative professors have found it useful, in considering Salinger, to discuss Beckett and Camus, Saul Bellow, and Martin Buber. And no doubt many other giants have been hitched to Salinger's wagon. Nor should we be surprised to learn that *The Catcher in the Rye* "is a masterpiece of symbolist fiction." There are even signs that the period of evaluation, such as it was, is over, and scholars can turn to source studies. One of our colleagues prints his speculations on the possibility of Sherwood Anderson's influence on Salinger. Confirmation of Salinger's place in the pantheon comes from an energetic German scholar who reviews over one hundred critics and concludes that Salinger has made it into the canon of American literature. Here is a fine chance for us to brush up on our German— what a reward for learning the language for our degrees!

Literary judgments of value are usually made tacitly, as assumptions, not logically argued. Merely to write about Salinger, to mention him in the same breath as Mark Twain or, heaven help us, Dostoevsky, is to make the claim for his place with the immortals. We must assume that these valuations are made in full sincerity. Many critics, like many readers, enjoyed *The Catcher in the Rye*, felt, in the reading, and in the remembering of the reading, the kind of satisfaction they had come to know as aesthetic pleasure. About their pleasure there is no room for dispute. One does not speculate, nowadays, in public, on one's colleagues' taste. But on the morning after, when mind awakes from its binge or its sleep, and pleasures are re-evaluated, criticism has its opportunity. The present critic leaps, no doubt bruising shins and egos, to seize it.

CATCHER FLATTERS THE READER

Beware of the novelists bearing gifts. The more delicious and enthralling the gifts, the more wary we must be. Best of the sweets Salinger has Holden giftwrap and deliver to us is the idea that to the degree that we like Holden Caulfield we were better than anyone who doesn't. The method of Salinger's flamboyant and insidious flattery goes like this: Line up all the people in the world who we, in our weakness, our failures of sympathy, our ignorance, our narrow-mindedness, have ever allowed ourselves to hate. Include in this line-up caricatures of people we know we should not have hated. (Once having hated them, we have a vested interest in seeing them worthy of hatred.) Include persons we hated because we knew they were better than we were. (There is nothing like jealousy to prompt and sustain hate.) Now introduce before that line-up a tortured, bleeding and sublimely "cute" victim of all the insults and injuries all of us have ever imagined ourselves to have suffered. Let this victim be on the edge of insanity, the result, of course, of what others have done to him. Let him ooze the sentimental notion that the doctrine of Original Sin, and all its modern parallels, have been revoked. This is crucial. Not only does it let our victim be perfect, it removes any excuse the evildoers might otherwise offer on their behalf. Let our victim believe that what the world needs now is not love, not even Coca-Cola, but that fool's gold, Sincerity. He himself has it of course, and some of it rubs off on his admirers, but no one else has it at all. Now the scene is set and the action commences. Blood in his eyes and trickling from his battered little nose, our victim raises a machine-gun and shoots everyone lined up before him. And he cries, weeps, as he does so. You see, utterly guilty as his tormentors are, he forgives them, he likes them! What super-human magnanimity! What delicious revenge, too! Who could resist enjoying this spectacle? Few have. . . .

SALINGER SEEMS TO AGREE WITH HOLDEN

We have no reason to assume that Salinger's attitudes differ from those of Holden Caulfield. It is the author's obligation to unmistakably untangle himself from his hero, or at least to give the reader the means to discover their relationship. But Salinger does neither. It seems absurd that a grown man, and a literate man at that, should hold the jejune opinions of Holden Caulfield. But he does and he lacks the grace or courage to say so outright, in or out of the novel. There isn't a whisper of any other view of life emanating from either quarter. We must take Salinger's silence in the novel to give consent. He is evidently angry that with the exception of himself—and his Holden—sincerity is in very short supply. "Then, after the Rockettes, a guy came out in a tuxedo and roller skates on, and started skating under a bunch of little tables, and telling jokes while he did it. He was a very good skater and all, but I couldn't enjoy it much because I kept picturing him practicing to be a guy that roller-skates on the stage" (ch. 18). Perfect sincerity requires and implies perfect spontaneity. And of course this utterly denies all the arts of life as well as the arts of Art. How does one know, Holden inquires, if the lawyer who has saved his client's life did so because "he really *wanted* to save guys' lives, or because . . . what [he] *really* wanted to do was to be a terrific lawyer, with everybody slapping [him] on the back and congratulating [him] in court when the goddam trial was over" (ch. 22). This is the question Holden asks of everyone. Its force is rhetorical. Holden wants a guarantee of the purity of human motive. He has been given everything else he wanted, but this complete absolution, of himself and his world, he cannot have. He cries "phoney," and takes up his bat and ball and leaves the game. We are to play by his rules or His Holiness will not play with us.

There is little point in using Salinger's text to show that Holden himself behaves with less than perfect kindness, less than Saintly sincerity. And to take that line against this novel is to accept its premise. *The Catcher in the Rye* urges the young to destroy their own, their only world, and to take refuge in their own soft dream-world peopled by themselves and by shadows of their perfected selves. No adolescent has ever entirely avoided this temptation. All of us had what used to be called "growing pains," fell into what used to be called a "brown study." Among the very rich, in our very rich country, all pleasures, no matter how self-deluding and self-defeating, no matter how selfish, are seized upon, and sold, and admired. Holden is a child of wealth, and most children wish they were too. The richer one is, the longer one may prolong one's adolescence. That is what Holden Caulfield is doing, and what Salinger and his admirers, are praising. Joan Didion comes to my aid here: She said that *Franny and Zooey* was "spurious" because of Salinger's "tendency to flatter the essential triviality within each of his readers." Its "appeal is precisely that it is self-help copy: it emerges finally as *Positive Thinking* for the upper middle classes, as *Double Your Energy and Live Without Fatigue* for Sarah Lawrence girls."

Those of us of a "certain age," brought up in the same streets and schools as Holden Caulfield, may be especially susceptible to Salinger's siren song. The present writer, along with a goodly percentage of our country's literati, shared Holden Caulfield's environment. We wondered about the ducks in Central Park lakes. We enjoyed a good cry about the sadness of life, the disappointments, the rain falling on our tennis courts. We too, in Salinger's most un-mean streets, discovered puberty, the painful way. But we managed to grow up, more or less; to see that it was not true, ever, that everybody was out of step but ourselves, to see that the words "compromise," "compassion," "tact," even "hypocrisy," were not obscenities which desecrated God's creation, but marks of the fact that none of us was, himself, God.

SALINGER PREVENTS US FROM SEEING *CATCHER* AS A COMEDY

Holden's youthful idealism, his bitterness toward the world he never made might have, had a Holden himself come before us, made for a successful novel. What could be funnier than the confessions of such a one as he? And while we would laugh at Holden, he would be laughing at us. How young we were, how charmingly silly. We could have had some good laughs, shed a tear for auld lang syne, shaken hands all round, and been on our way. But Salinger's Holden Caulfield is made of soggy cardboard. The death of his younger brother Allie hangs over his story forbidding anyone in it more than a momentary laugh. That death, utterly unrelated to the vapid social criticism which is Holden's prime activity, should have made Holden atypical, a special case whose opinions may be regarded only as pointers to his private distress. But Salinger ignores this; evidently he wants Holden's opinions on the general condition of society to be highly regarded, and he wants no one involved, character, author, reader, critic, to see his story as a comedy. We must, out of courtesy, courtesy that has been uncourteously forced upon us, take it all with high seriousness. Salinger needs the dead Allie in his novel so that we may not laugh. Yet the story itself is the quintessential comedy, the story of maturity looking back, with a wince and a smile and a guffaw at its own immaturity.

No character of Holden Caulfield is the only certifiable "phoney" in the novel. No youth, no matter how emotionally shaken, goes so long, so seriously single-mindedly after his real and imagined enemies. When the real Holden Caulfields encounter the terrors, such as they are, of their gilded ghettoes, they stumble every now and then on those insights which will add up to their definition of being grown-up. Not Holden. His larger considerations are bogus. He meanders about as if he were free to find out about things for himself, free to stumble on the other sides of the "phoney" question, to learn why people behave the way they do. But Salinger has put blinders around the boy. He never learns anything; never considers anything antagonistic to his sustaining faith that everything and everybody is wrong. It is as if Holden grew up at the knee of Abbie Hoffman—but even that is more funny than true. No matter how doctrinaire the upbringing, bright boys have a way of seeing around the blinders their elders set in place. But then Holden is not a real boy at all; he is Salinger's dream-boy, the boy who will not grow up. He is immaturity's best defense, a non-stop assault on maturity.

CATCHER IS AN INSULT TO CHILDHOOD

But after all this we really should petition the court to reduce the charge brought against Mr. Salinger. Boys being what we know them to be, despite the example of Holden, the crime is not impairment of the morals of a minor, but only attempted impairment. No real harm will be done by this book, unless professors succeed in making it a classic. *The Catcher in the Rye* is no more than an insult to all boys, to us who have been boys, and to the girls and ex-girls too. It is an insult to childhood and to adulthood. It is an insult to our ideas of civilization, to our ideal land in which ladies and gentlemen try to grow up, try to find and save their dignity.

CHRONOLOGY

1919

Jerome David Salinger born January 1 in New York City.

1936

Graduates from Valley Forge Military Academy.

1937–1938

Travels to Austria and Poland; attends Ursinus College and New York University.

1939

Enrolls in writing course at Columbia University with Whit Burnett; World War II begins in Europe.

1940

Publishes first short story, "The Young Folks," in Burnett's literary magazine, *Story*.

1941

Pearl Harbor attack; United States enters World War II.

1942–1945

Drafted, serves in the Army Signal Corps and the Counter-Intelligence Corps.

1944

Lands on Utah Beach on D-day.

1945

World War II ends; Salinger marries Frenchwoman named Sylvia (maiden name unknown).

1946

United Nations holds first session; Salinger divorces.

1948–1949

Berlin blockade and airlift.

1950

Senator Joseph McCarthy launches hunt for communists in the U.S. government; begins what is later called the Red Scare; *My Foolish Heart* (film adaptation of "Uncle Wiggily in Connecticut") released.

1951

Catcher in the Rye published in United States; British edition released without photograph or biography; Rosenbergs sentenced to death for espionage against the United States.

1952

Dwight D. Eisenhower elected president; Salinger retires to house in Cornish, New Hampshire.

1953

Nine Stories published, reaches number one on the *New York Times* best-seller list; Salinger gives one of his last published interviews to high school student Shirley Blaney.

1955

Marries Claire Douglas on February 17; daughter Margaret Ann Salinger born December 10.

1960

Son, Matthew, born; John F. Kennedy elected president.

1961

Catcher tops 1.5 million in sales.

1964–1975

American involvement in Vietnam War.

1965

Salinger's last published work, "Hapworth 16, 1924"; *Catcher* sales hit 5 million.

1967

Divorces Claire Douglas.

1970

Repays, with interest, advance received from Little, Brown.

1974

Unauthorized, pirated collection, *The Complete Uncollected Stories of J.D. Salinger*, published.

1975

Over 9 million copies of *Catcher* sold.

1986

Salinger blocks publication of Ian Hamilton's *J.D. Salinger: A Writing Life* due to the inclusion of unpublished letters; *Catcher* continues to sell at a rate of twenty to thirty thousand copies a month.

1988

Ian Hamilton publishes *In Search of J.D. Salinger*, without the letters in question.

1996

Salinger's literary agents force "The Holden Server," a *Catcher in the Rye* website, to shut down because signing on to the site randomly generates quotes from the book.

1997

Salinger to republish "Hapworth 16, 1924."

FOR FURTHER RESEARCH

ABOUT *THE CATCHER IN THE RYE*

Norbert Blei, "'If You Want to Know the Truth...' *The Catcher in the Rye.*" In *Censored Books: Critical Viewpoints*, Nicholas J. Karolides et al., eds. Metuchen, NJ: Scarecrow, 1993.

Harold Bloom, ed., *Holden Caulfield*. New York: Chelsea House, 1990.

Adam Green, "If Holden Caulfield Spent a Week in Today's Manhattan," *New York Times*, December 23, 1995.

Sanford Pinsker, The Catcher in the Rye: *Innocence Under Pressure*. New York: Twayne, 1993.

William Riggan, "The Naif," *Pícaros, Madmen, Naïfs, and Clowns: The Unreliable First-Person Narrator*. Norman: University of Oklahoma Press, 1981.

Gerald Rosen, *Zen in the Art of J.D. Salinger*. Berkeley, CA: Creative Arts, 1977.

Joel Salzberg, ed., *Critical Essays on Salinger's* The Catcher in the Rye. Boston: Hall, 1990.

Jack Salzman, ed., *New Essays on* The Catcher in the Rye. Cambridge: Cambridge University Press, 1991.

Jack R. Sublette, *J.D. Salinger: An Annotated Bibliography: 1938–1981*. New York: Garland, 1984.

ABOUT J.D. SALINGER

Warren French, *J.D. Salinger, Revisited*. Boston: Twayne, 1988.

Henry A. Grunwald, ed., *Salinger: A Critical and Personal Portrait*. New York: Harper, 1962.

Ian Hamilton, *In Search of J.D. Salinger.* New York: Random House, 1988.

Ernest Havemann, "The Search for the Mysterious J.D. Salinger," *Life,* November 3, 1961.

William Maxwell, "J.D. Salinger," *Book of the Month Club News,* midsummer 1951.

James E. Miller Jr., ed., *J.D. Salinger.* Minneapolis: University of Minneapolis Press, 1965.

ABOUT THE 1950s

David Halberstam, *The Fifties.* New York: Random House, 1993.

Karal Ann Marling, *As Seen on TV: The Visual Culture of Everyday Life in the 1950s.* Cambridge, MA: Harvard University Press, 1994.

Douglas T. Miller, *The Fifties: The Way We Really Were.* New York: Doubleday, 1977.

James T. Patterson, ed., *Grand Expectations: The United States 1945–1974.* Oxford: Oxford University Press, 1996.

WORKS BY J.D. SALINGER

"The Young Folks" in *Story;* "Go See Eddie" in *University of Kansas City Review* (1940)

"The Hang of It" in *Collier's;* "The Heart of a Broken Story" in *Esquire* (1941)

"The Long Debut of Lois Taggett" in *Story;* "Personal Notes of an Infantryman" in *Collier's* (1942)

"The Varioni Brothers" in *Saturday Evening Post* (1943)

"Both Parties Concerned" in *Saturday Evening Post;* "Soft-Boiled Sergeant" in *Saturday Evening Post;* "Last Day of the Last Furlough" in *Saturday Evening Post;* "Once a Week Won't Kill You" in *Story* (1944)

"A Boy in France" in *Saturday Evening Post;* "Elaine" in *Story;* "This Sandwich Has No Mayonnaise" in *Esquire;* "The Stranger" in *Collier's;* "I'm Crazy" in *Collier's* (1945)

"Slight Rebellion Off Madison" in *New Yorker* (1946)

"A Young Girl in 1941 with No Waist at All" in *Mademoiselle;* "The Inverted Forest" in *Cosmopolitan* (1947)

"A Girl I Knew" in *Good Housekeeping;* "Blue Melody" in *Cosmopolitan;* "A Perfect Day for Bananafish" in *New Yorker;* "Uncle Wiggily in Connecticut" in *New Yorker;* "Just Before the War with the Eskimos" in *New Yorker* (1948)

"The Laughing Man" in *New Yorker;* "Down at the Dinghy" in *Harper's* (1949)

"For Esmé—with Love and Squalor" in *New Yorker* (1950)

The Catcher in the Rye; "Pretty Mouth and Green My Eyes" in *New Yorker* (1951)

"De Daumier-Smith's Blue Period" in *World Review* (1952)

"Teddy" in *New Yorker; Nine Stories* (1953)

"Franny" in *New Yorker;* "Raise High the Roofbeam, Carpenters" in *New Yorker* (1955)

"Zooey" in *New Yorker* (1957)

"Seymour: An Introduction" in *New Yorker* (1959)

Franny and Zooey (1961)

Raise High the Roofbeam, Carpenters and Seymour: An Introduction (1963)

"Hapworth 16, 1924" in *New Yorker* (1965)

INDEX

WITHDRAWN